...Memoirs And Confessions

Of A

Stage Magician

by

Donald & Joyce Brandon

Published By

TAG PUBLICATIONS

Library of Congress Catalog Card Number 95-61911

ISBN 0-964890-0-6

PHOTO CREDITS

Donald Estes, Jr., Renee Pace, T. Mack Reynolds,
Richard Krudwig, and the scores of others from
over the last 100 years whose identities are unkown.

POSTERS

Colorcraft, Oklahoma City; Neal Walters Showprints,
Eureaka Springs, Arkansas; Pico Showprints, Los Angeles;
Globe Poster Printing Corporation, Baltimore, Maryland;
and General Art and Process Company, San Antonio.

TYPESETTING

Uecker Enterprises, Richmond, Virginia.

COVER DESIGNS

Joyce Brandon

"IT IS NOT ABOUT BEING A
YOUNG MAGICIAN, OR OLD,
IT IS NOT YOUTHFUL. IT IS
WHAT MAGIC HAS TO BE IN
ORDER TO BE GOOD!"
-Author Unknown

TABLE OF CONTENTS

i

INTRODUCTION

This book came about as a direct result of badgering and harassing my husband over a period of many years. He had told me so many of these stories, usually late at night, as we traveled from place to place with the show. It seemed so sad to let all of these pages of people die.

Don has a fabulous memory for details. He shared some wonderful moments with a lot of terrific (and some not so) people. I thought that they should be saved so this book is a sort of "life raft" for them.

Back in the '20's South Texas (contrary to the idea portrayed with the saloon evident in most cowboy movies) was dry. This caused Don's father to choose his path. Born in the same neighborhood and at times even living on the same street with Harry Willard and his family started Don on his.

Willard the Wizard was a fabulous magician who was ingenious, original, cantankerous and Don truly loved him. He was like Santa Claus to a little boy and later became Don's mentor, his teacher and his friend. Their story intertwines in Don's early years because of the friendship between Willard and Don's grandfather, Charlie Miller, plus the fact that Don's father was absent when he had one at all. These things will be covered in the story.

Don suffered from asthma, hayfever, and allergies all of his life. Many of his young endeavors were controlled by his physical condition. Although he was not diagnosed as having Diabetes Mellitus until his late twenties, I do believe that he was suffering from that disease for many years prior to its discovery, perhaps all his life, which is evidenced by the damage to all of his organs. Many days his health problems left him almost helpless. Two of the greatest practitioners of real magic are Dr. Foster Jennings, his cardiologist and Dr. Timothy Wolfgang, his cardiovascular surgeon who brought him through three heart procedures in 1994. This gave Don the opportunity to write some of his adventures and misadventures. Guilt, too, played a part... he always felt guilty for not living up to his mother's expectations, especially since she worked so hard and literally worried herself sick. He felt that he let Harry Willard down too by not carrying on in the tradition of Willard and his famous family. Aside from health problems, Cinemascope was the kiss of death for motion picture theatres that had been presenting live stage shows because it sealed off the stages... forever and those stages had been the route that Don traveled.

One person was always encouraging and helpful to us throughout the years, whether grabbing her Nikon and rushing to take pictures or donning a costume to fill a role in the show, at the last minute. She could round up a crew and cast after we had exhausted every avenue and she would always be there with her beautiful smiling face. As Willard would have said a genuine "thee-at--i-cal" person. WE MISS HER!

Dedicated to our daughter
Renée Alexis Pace
November 5, 1951-August 5, 1990.

JOYCE BRANDON

Chapter 1

WHEN IT ALL STARTED....

I suppose that the best place to commence is at the beginning. Being born at a very early age I am sure there is much that I am unable to remember; but, perhaps there is enough to render this a worthwhile read.

I was born in San Antonio, Texas, and was, pretty much, raised by my grandparents, an uncle, my mother (who had to be absent much of the time because of her work) and, in no small part, by the influence of Harry Willard.

The year was 1936. I gave my first magical performance and it was a nightmare. I strung up some old blankets on a clothesline wire in a combination garage/barn. That was my stage. The tricks, made of mostly cardboard and paper, simply refused to work in the manner which I had envisioned. As a matter of fact, I recall that only two tricks worked. I was going to do the vanishing rabbit trick. I did not have a rabbit so I borrowed the next door neighbor's cat. The cat knew nothing of my theatrical aspirations and cared even less. We had a cardboard box with a hole in the bottom large enough for the rabbit to drop through. There was a stiff loose piece of cardboard the size of the bottom of the box, that acted like a flap. It was to drop down and cover the hole in the bottom after I dropped the cat through to my cousin who was hiding under the box. We had hell catching the cat. More hell dropping him in the hole into the waiting arms of Charley. The cat went crazy, tore holes in the sheet, exposed the presence of Charley, knocked the table over and I spent the next 55 years hating cats. The rabbit/cat trick was NOT one of the tricks that worked. After the show, members of my audience--which totaled about seven--wanted their pennies back that they had paid as an admission price. A fight ensued over that. I decided not to give any more performances until I had "perfected" my program...somewhat.

Earlier I said that I hated cats for the next 55 years. That was kind of true, but I should have said that I hated cats until I met "Annie" who is our Turkish Angoran. We found each other many years ago and I fell madly in love with her. I adore her now and always will.

I am getting ahead of myself. I think it best that I explain what was behind all of this magic business in the first place. My father was never around; he was busy serving time in the Federal Correctional Facility at El Reno, Oklahoma. It was a five-year sentence for violation of the Volstead Act (Prohibition). He had been a rather successful dinner, dancing, gambling night club operator for years but the need for booze in his establishments and the lure of great profits managed to convince him to start buying large quantities of alcohol over in old Mexico. There he would smuggle the liquor across the border. The alcohol was in ten-gallon cans. It was easy to bribe the border guards and he always had a man with a legitimate law enforcement badge with him. He would pour the alcohol into one-fifth gallon bottles. He would color it, cap it, and seal it. I remember him telling me that he paid about 25¢ per gallon for the alcohol in Mexico and sold it for about $15 per gallon in Texas.

He enjoyed a very peaceful relationship with the law because his partner was the Sheriff of Bexar County, Texas. What actually did him in was a gloomy night following a border crossing, he and the sheriff saw a roadblock outside the town of Cuero, Texas. Federal agents were waiting to apprehend the culprits. My grandmother, who was a religious fanatic, had called the authorities and alerted them. My father saw the roadblock up ahead and both men decided to avoid capture by running through the fields and brush, across

2

country, to another road. They made a pact in which it was agreed that if one were caught and the other got away, the "free" man would take care of the others family and do everything possible to free the one charged. The sheriff was short and fat; my father was lean, mean, and athletic. My father, being far in the lead, ran straight into the arms of the agents. He told them that he was operating alone. The sheriff got away and he kept his word; he helped my mother and me. Further he bribed a guard to smuggle in parts of a gun, one at a time, to my father who reassembled the weapon in his cell and taped it under a wash basin. Then he called the warden and took him over to the location and showed him the gun. He said, "someone must be planning an escape with this gun." They let my father out of the prison after just a few months for "good behavior." Meanwhile my mother had divorced him...for the first time.

I had substitute fathers. The favorite of which was my grandfather Charles Franklin Miller. My grandfather, "Charley," was a school teacher in Atascosa County and he was a "scientific" blacksmith. This was a term applied to those with the special knowledge of being able to correct malfunctions in the gait of a horse by changing the horseshoes...sometimes a lighter shoe, or a heavier one. Sometimes the shoe had to be higher on one side or the other. Perhaps it had to be raised at the back or lowered. It got to be pretty technical stuff.

Before horse racing was outlawed in Texas we had a racetrack in San Antonio that was known as "Alamo Downs." My grandfather had, almost, continually worked with the race horses during the season. He maintained his blacksmith shop in the 5000 block of South Flores Street. Directly across the street he, my grandmother, and my uncle, operated a meat market and grocery store. Behind the store was the house in which we lived. Behind that was the house where Alma Ketchum lived; she was a chiropractor. She would give me "adjustments" when I was having a bad attack of asthma. I do not think these treatments helped, but it was a comfort to my folks who worried about me a great deal. Alma died of tuberculosis. In those days most people called TB "consumption." It is probably an amazing thing that I did not catch it from her because I understand that it is contagious. One day along came antibiotics and that seemed to stop TB. Vast numbers of people died from asthma until they found that

3

adrenaline could halt bronchospasms. I was terribly underweight along with the asthma and always looked near death so my family catered to me because of my ill health. I forgot to mention that it was Alma Ketchum's cat that was the unwilling star of my vanishing rabbit act.

A fellow would come in the grocery store on a daily basis when he was in town. His name was Harry Willard. *(See Appendix A-1)* After he bought staples and meat and groceries for his "cook house" (for the 35 people working for him), he would say to my grandfather, "come on Charley, let's go up the street." I knew what that meant--to really go over to the Mulberry Inn and have a pitcher of beer (it was James Mitchell's Place before and I do not know what year the name was changed). If my grandfather was not in the grocery store Willard would come over to his shop and get him. The two men would then proceed to spend the rest of the evening drinking and telling each other how smart they were. The more they drank, the smarter they got. Frequently, they would scheme out a plan to make a new "trick" and stumble over to my grandfather's shop and proceed to build it. Some great magic came out of that shop. Between my grandfather's metal work ability and Willard's prowess with hammer and saw the two of them could make most anything. Harry Willard was a magician. Maybe that is not sufficient. It would be more correct if I said that he was "THE MAGICIAN."

on Beatrice Street. We had three bedrooms, bath, kitchen, dining room, porch, and washroom across the back.

Willard's house was at 315 Truax Street. Truax was one block north of the intersection of Theo Avenue and S. Flores. Truax did not cross S. Flores...it stopped there. The lot at 317 Truax was where the barns were and the Willard equipment. When the trucks were unloaded they were taken out in the country and left on a friend's farm until the show went on the road again. My aunt Ollie and Pinky lived at 319 Truax. *(See Appendix A-2)*

Chapter 2

AN ATTEMPT AT
SOME CLARIFICATION

Originally the Shadowland Night Club was at 121 1/2 Soledad Street. Rolla Estes got the bright idea to move this club outside of the City limits in order to avoid having to deal with the local police. That way the only ones with whom he had to contend was the County Sheriff (his partner) and the Feds. Shadowland was moved way out to 13445 Old Blanco Road.

Rolla also owned the Chicken Plantation. This was a posh gambling, dinner and night club. Both Shadowland and the Chicken Plantation became the two most notorious speakeasy's in San Antonio. He also had the Turf Bar on Losoya Street; I think that the street number was 224. I also believe that the name of Losoya Street changed to South Broadway at the same time they tore down the Palace Theatre. The Chicken Plantation was located out in the County on the old Corpus Christi Highway. The Mulberry Inn was at 4902 S. Flores Street. The blacksmith shop was at 4910 S. Flores. The grocery and market was at 5003 S. Flores.

Aunt Drussie and Uncle Ed's Ice House was at 5007 S. Flores. Their little house was across S. Flores behind Caskey's Service Station

Now this is a very thin table with beautiful ornate legs that sits in the center of the stage. The lady assistant walks out and lays down on the table. A sheet is thrown over her, some inflammable is added and the sheet is set afire. When the fire dies down all that is left, in the ashes, is the skeleton. Harry really wanted to stage this in a big way. He had special costumes made that were harem style for the girls and pantaloons with sashes worn bare chestedly and with a fez for the men. Special music and huge oriental ostrich plume fans made it look very elegant. The trick is done with a mirror that runs the length of the table that drops down, at the appropriate time to a 45° angle and it reflects the floor but audiences think they are seeing underneath to the backdrop because there is a floor covering that matches the rear curtain.

The very first performance of this "miracle" was the last. It was a disaster. Harry owned a big Russian Wolfhound which he dearly loved. The girl came onstage and climbed up on the table and the secret mirror dropped down. Before anyone could stop him, the dog walked across the stage, up to the mirror, looked at himself, lifted his hind leg and urinated on the mirror, whereupon he calmly walked off the stage. What the audience saw was the most striking feat of all because it appeared that two dogs, one walking across the stage, and the other "magically" walking across the backdrop stopped, touched noses, urinated on each other and then walked off the stage. Harry was mortified and pushed the illusion off the stage and never did the trick again.

The elastic lady illusion posed problems dating back to when its creator first introduced it. Selbit was a very original thinker when it came to inventing stage magic. In his elastic lady a girl is placed in upright stocks, front doors to the huge cabinet are closed, her hands are passed through large slot openings into more stocks and her hands and feet are apparently stretched twelve feet from her torso. This is accomplished by having two additional girls concealed in trick compartments inside of the cabinet proper. In the Selbit version the two extra girls were hidden in pontoon-like compartments, one of which was at each end of the cabinet. These compartments were virtually invisible with their flat black felt covering up against a flat black backdrop. Even when the lighting was perfect these hiding places left a great deal to be desired. More often than not these "gimmicks" exposed the trick. There are several versions of this mystery in use today. Willard had three or four of this trick. He was not crazy about any of them. He built one of his own that employed the most unique method I have ever seen. His illusion base (platform) could actually, when he so desired, hide four women. Including the lady to be stretched, this trick required five ladies and five men. The base (platform) could be measured at ends, as well as the middle, and was only four inches thick. It did not bulge or thicken anyplace. Willard seemed to stretch the lady's limbs twelve feet apart. Then her head would drop to the floor of the platform and Willard would take the lady by the hair and twist her head around and around in a complete 360° rotation which brought the house down because the whole thing seemed so absurd.

A massive fire literally destroyed the Willard show as I had known it as a boy. True he had other shows stashed in storage, with various friends around the country but that magnificent theatre of canvas could not be replaced. Harry called Ben Davenport, owner of Dailey Brothers Circus. Ben sent Harry trucks, seating, lights, and sound but no costumes or canvas. Si Rubens, owner of Rogers Brothers Circus sent Harry another tent. It was a circus style with centerpoles down the middle which obstructed the view of the stage. Audiences did not have an opportunity to see the stage without some sort of a big pole in the way. This hurt and it hurt badly. The show never regained its momentum. Harry was diagnosed with tuberculosis in 1951 and went to the Woodmen of World hospital out on North New Braunfels Avenue in San Antonio. He remained in that facility for two years. Shortly after he was released and pronounced cured, his wife, Joy, was diagnosed with cancer. Surgery was largely ineffective; she died a few months later.

Chapter 4

LOOKING AT THE WILLARD SHOW THROUGH A CHILD'S EYES... AND OTHERS

Willard had given my grandfather a bunch of free tickets to see the world famous "WILLARD THE WIZARD" show. My family took me to that performance. As a matter of fact they took me at my insistence to see the show every third night for a month. That was, primarily, because the giant full-evening show was completely different every third day. This really remarkable traveling theatre could set up in a city and remain there for a period of six weeks and give a complete change of program so often that it created a following of tremendous proportions.

Although Willard made a few nationwide tours in theaters and auditoriums, his prime thrust was in his own tented theatre. This was actually a tent within a tent with an air space between layers. This kept it cooler in summer and warmer in winter. The giant fans with six foot blades were each mounted in one, or another, of the shows huge semi-trailers. These trailers were backed up all around the periphery of the tent's side walls. When the trucks were unloaded, if necessary, huge cakes of ice could be placed in the trailers and the

11

fans could blow the cold air into the innermost tent for really fantastic cooling. This was even before refrigeration air conditioning as we now know it. This worked for warming in very cold weather using coal as the heat source and the fans for air power.

When a person walked into this arrangement they would feel as if they were in one of the really fine theaters. There was red carpet down the aisles, folding padded chairs with individual chair covers affording 1500 seats. There was a "blue" section of "jacks and stringers" for cheaper seating at the rear and restrooms. In the "lobby" concessions were available but no one was allowed to take food or drink into the "auditorium" proper. The roof happened to be suspended by strange things known as "A-Frame supports." This avoided the center poles which are usually running down the middle of a circus tent. Willard would not permit center poles because they would obstruct the vision of the patrons. The stage was complete and could accommodate up to thirty scenic background drops in addition to the "grand" curtain, the "olio," "legs" (wings, borders, etc.).

The show generally had its own orchestra, its own lights via two 15,000 KW generators, a cook tent with seating for the entire crew, a costume tent separated for men and women. There was a small animal tent for the livestock.

To illustrate the power of the operation, Harry Willard took his show into downtown Oklahoma City on a very large parking lot across from the Warner theatre. Night after night, during the worst part of the depression, Willard played to full houses for six weeks while the Warner was lucky to have a couple of dozen in the audience. Willard came through that era with a great deal of money. On opening night, he would insist that everyone pay for admission. At intermission he would step out in front of the curtain and say, "Now ladies and gentlemen you have seen the value of our show. We will be here for six weeks and present a completely different show of the same quality every third night. We will bring you a new show every three days...you must bring yourselves. We know how difficult our economy is right now; we know that you folks are low on money and many of you have none at all. We know that you need to escape, if only for a few hours, from your worries. We can help you do that. So if you do not have the price of admission, it's alright. I have 35 people working on this show and for the life of me I do not know why, but all of them want to eat every day. So bring whatever you can spare, a chicken, jar of preserves, loaf of bread, fresh vegetables or whatever...just drop it off at the box office and you will be given a seat." So many days that you would not want to try to count them, Willard would take a truckload of poultry and/or produce to the local market for sale. He always carried a money belt under his shirt with $4,000 in it all the time. Today that would be like $400,000 or more.

To explain just how well liked Harry Willard was, he was the only human being in history ever allowed to actually set up and operate a tented theatre on the Capitol grounds in Baton Rouge, Louisiana, for the express purpose of presenting a magic show to the general public. He was a close personal friend of Huey Long. He was known as, and treated like, a god in the State of Louisiana.

Harry Willard was one of three brothers. The other two, Tommy and Robert, each had shows that were practically identical to Harry's...that is with one exception. Harry would take each trick and build others with different methods of operation. If you saw him perform a stunt one night and wanted to come back the next night to see if you could "catch on" to how it was done, you would find that you came away even more mystified.

Tommy Willard was killed in a train accident and Robert died in Canada. The shows were equally successful. Harry's father and grandfather were magicians. His great grandfather was supposedly the Irish Court magician in Ireland.

The only theatrical enterprise that could approach the Willard extravaganza would be "Justinani" the South American magician. The "Justinani" show was not even close due to the vastness of the Willard dynasty. The Willard show, at one point, was actually larger than the Barnum and Bailey Circus. It took 31 semi-trucks just to move the show.

Never having seen the show, I nevertheless, had some idea of what it was because I would spend most of my evenings after school at my Aunt "Ollie's" house. Olive Haggin, and her mother "Pinky," were my aunt and great aunt, respectively, and they lived next to the open yard (lot) that was part of the Willard home. Sometimes, in the middle of the night if I happened to be staying over, I would be awakened by a long line of trucks out front. Many still had their lights on, unloading crates and materials next door. Willard was back in town.

Since my grandparents had to keep the store open until at least 10 o'clock every evening, I would stay at my aunt's house until they came for me, and frequently would spend the night. My natural association with matters Willard was a normal consequence of the this closeness and Harry's friendship with my grandfather. Not my grandmother. Her name was Mary King Miller. She came from the King family that originally created the well-known King Ranch in South Texas. She was really crazy over religion. The members of her family were mostly very gifted musicians. Mary could play many instruments well--the guitar (standard) as her preferred instrument. Her brother Dee King played both violin and bass. Her other brother, Will, played the piano and sax. They played together as an orchestra but never professionally. She would only tolerate church and Christmas songs with the exception of one number..."After the Ball." I never did figure that one out. She hated Willard and said that he was in league with the Devil and refused me any association with him or members of his family. That certainly did not stop me. I think that the real basis for her hatred of Harry was the fact that he and my grandfather were best drinking buddies. She accused Willard of leading my granddad astray. I never believed that. At best they led each other.

On more than one occasion Harry Willard told me, "I got drunk 35 years ago and never have sobered up." He was a real miracle when it came to drinking hard liquor. That man would down a fifth of Irish whiskey everyday together with copious quantities of beer. His wife, Joy, drank Vodka or Gin in almost the same amounts. It made no difference how much he drank. Once he was dressed in his white tie and tails, he would walk out on the stage and give a full two-hour performance that was, undoubtedly, the most delightful, enchanting, funny, mystifying performance in showbusiness. He would subsequently walk back off the stage and collapse. When he would wake up he would say, "May I please have a drink...Irish whiskey will do just fine."

Willard's first wife, Carlotta (Lottie) died after the birth of their son Howard and daughter Rosemary. Lottie's maiden name was Katzmark. Her brother Paul Katzmark went to school with my

14

mother. They dated for a while and were getting pretty serious. My mother backed off...I never knew why. I think she seemed to appreciate excitement, perhaps even danger, more than Paul could ever provide. I think she was attracted to my father because of his somewhat unsavory reputation as a gambler and night club operator. She had been pretty serious about several other fellows--one of which was Guido Dittmar. I will tell you more about the Dittmar's later because that is a story in itself.

Willard was small, very small, in stature but, was still viewed by most as a giant. He had broad shoulders and virtually no hips. In tails, he looked like a wedge of cheese. He had a friend named Harry Blackstone Senior. Both Blackstone and Willard were considered THE premiere magic maestros. I think the one thing they had in common was their voices. This was what overwhelmed and electrified audiences. Even more so than the really fabulous magic and illusions which they performed. Very, very, large audiences could hear them in the upper balconies without microphones. That voice would crackle through the house like lightning. There was one other magician of that period who achieved legendary status. His name was "Dante." His real name was Harry Jansen. Even Jansen, who was well-known worldwide, did not have the voice of Blackstone and Willard. He was very good but simply did not cause an audience to feel as if they were compelled as did Blackstone and Willard. Notwithstanding all of this while at a magic meeting in Louisiana Harry Blackstone, speaking of Willard, said, "Lord, God, how I wish I could do what that man does!"

At one time both Willard and Blackstone were billed as the same show. Each used the name of "Frederik the Great." A magician billing himself as "Frederik" had a very, very large amount of beautiful colored posters and billing materials, including 24 sheet billboards, printed. FREDERIK promptly went broke; the printer wanted his money. Willard and Blackstone went in together, bought the paper, and divided the materials. Blackstone agreed to stay in the north while using that title and Willard the south. It worked out very well.

15

Chapter 5

SOME THINGS ABOUT
MY FAMILY, ME, AND OTHERS

I think that the primary reason my mother divorced my father was that she feared when he was released from prison he would somehow manage to borrow some money against--or sell--the home. She had purchased a two-story Victorian home that was across the street from where millionaire's row began. It offered a somewhat prestigious location on the northside and was a small block from the gorgeous San Pedro Park with its natural springs emitting several hundreds of thousands of gallons of water daily. This water ran through a natural swimming pool that was over two city blocks long.

My mother, Nancy Jewell Miller, added onto this house and converted it into five apartments. *(See Appendix A-3)* It was stately in appearance with its four cream columns that were two stories high. Two tall cedar trees, manicured hedges, and grass graced the front. The house itself was also cream colored and trimmed in an unusual burnt orange color. New awnings in bright green, orange, black, tan, and white could be raised or lowered on every window. These apartments attracted attorneys, judges, doctors, dentists, and business people who appreciated living in that area. Despite all we could do, we still almost lost the house because of an inability to keep up with the mortgage payments. Had it not been for Franklin Roosevelt's election as President of the United States and his subsequent emergency legislation passing a moratorium preventing foreclosures for a reasonable period of time, that house would have been gone. For the many years that I lived with my grandparents we could not live in our apartment house because it took all of the rents, and then some, to meet the financial obligations.

My father, Rolla Estes, did get out of prison after a few months and did return. Whereupon my mother remarried him. That proved to be a mistake which she again rectified, rather quickly I might add.

Between the two times that my mother married and divorced my father, she was briefly married to a man named Edward Newman. Little is known about him and the only reason I mention the matter is to illustrate the fact that my mother was married five times in all. Several years after the last divorce from my father, she married Albert W. Jeffreys and we went to live in his home town of Herrin, Illinois. While there I met, on several occasions, Mr. Will Lindhorst who was known publicly as, "Chandu the Magician." He had a weekly nationwide radio broadcast based on the character of "Chandu" which, for millions of youngsters, was very mysterious, exciting, and adventuresome. I also made frequent trips to Chicago and on to Colon, Michigan, home of Abbott's Magic Company. The peculiar thing about my mother's marriages was that she felt that whatever her married name happened to be at the time was the last name that I should also use. This curtailed the raising of eyebrows but played holy hell with school records, Social Security, correspondences of long standing, etc.

As I recall it was in Marion, Illinois, that I saw Ed Reno. Marion is about thirty miles west of Herrin. I had ridden a bus over and Mr. Reno was to perform in a local school. He arrived late and I offered to help him carry his equipment onto the stage which turned out to be two long flights of stairs up. I never saw so many old broken boxes, suitcases, and junk in my life. By the time it was all on stage I had about decided my trip was in vain. Mr. Reno had shoes that were scuffed up and his coat was frayed. His hat looked like he slept in it. Still I waited around for the show. The curtain opened and

I never saw such terrific looking equipment and I never saw a better one man show. I felt like a damn fool. I learned a great lesson that has been around for a long time--never, never, NEVER judge a book by its cover.

When we returned to San Antonio, I had accumulated enough equipment for a full evening show. I am not sure how it came about, but I was booked to give an assembly show performance for the student body and an evening show that night for the PTA. My show was to be held in the auditorium of Edgewood Junior High School. We were living with my mother's other brother, Largen Miller, on Peach Street. All of our apartments were full and we could not live there until such time as one of the tenants vacated. This was generally quite a while. For some reason our tenants seemed to stay...frequently for years.

I had my equipment in garages at the apartment house and at my grandparents who now lived on a farm out on Division Avenue. First thing I did was look up Willard to seek his counsel, guidance, and advice. To which he gave his often heard reply, "Hey Bud...come on let's go get a beer." Several pitchers of beer later Harry not only advised me but wanted to go along to the show. I had two other assistants. Frank Lassiter and Leo Harper who were both school mates. Harry took his truck and we carted all my junk over to the school the day before the big show. The principal was so cooperative that he let us have exclusive use of the auditorium and even gave us a key so that we might rehearse the night before. Since I had helped Harry so many times on his show, perhaps he wanted to repay what he considered favors by me. All I ever did for him was backstage work. I was always too tall to work on stage with Harry. I literally towered over him. The next day both shows came off extremely well. I do not know if I was trying to impress Harry or that his presence made things go smooth. Harry worked the curtains, lights, sound... everything. Tommy Cheeseman was in the audience that night. Tommy was stationed at Kelly Air Force Base and his home was in Bethlehem, Pennsylvania. Cheeseman was with Special Services and attached to the Air Force. He was staring in "Let's Take Off," the all military cast that entertained troops all over. I became the only civilian member of that show.

That led to my inclusion as a permanent member of the troupe

18

on Al Ohliger's unit of camp shows. These shows went all over a second time. We were in the mountain snows, the desert heat, the torrential rain, the mud and usually did not even know where we had been. Traveling mostly in the dark of night over treacherous dirt roads and terrain not fit for man nor beast, we performed in the back of half tracks, boxing rings, hangars, open fields, etc. I came away both hating and loving it. I developed a great disrespect for military matters and great suspicion of government in general.

Tommy Cheeseman was a real "show biz kid." He, too, had grown up around theatrical business. Tommy was primarily a dancer. He was a fine actor and vocalist but as far as eccentric and acrobatic tap were concerned he ranked along with such luminaries as Donald O'Connor, Johnny Coy, Leo Gorcey (later well known in "B" films for his portrayal of the leader of the "Dead End Kids") and Sammy Davis, Jr. during the years of the Will Mastin Trio. He was not "top rung" like Kelly and Astaire but came in a very good second. As a result of his shocking red hair, which looked like it was on fire, audiences found themselves looking at his head more that his feet. That probably isn't too good for a dancer. We hit it off and Tommy kept trying to convince me to come back east with him where he and his family had connections. I did not believe that I should have to rely on the "good old boy" network in order to be successful. I strongly believed that "talent will out." How wrong I was.

Chapter 6

MORE ABOUT MY GRANDFATHER...

In my grandfather's shop (Charlie Miller's Blacksmith Shop) the men working there were usually paid at the end of the day on Friday. I always called my grandfather "Pappy." From this juncture on I will try and do that for the sake of brevity. There ranged anywhere from three to sixteen workers in the shop depending on how many big jobs had been contracted.

Pappy had an employee named "Pee Wee." I never knew his real name. I think that Pappy gave him work because he felt sorry for his family. Pee Wee had a terrible reputation in the community. He was a giant of a man--stood well over six feet tall and had a highly muscled body to accompany his height. Sober, you never met a nicer person. When Pee Wee drank, locals closed and bolted their doors. He had put a number of people in the hospital and I think at one time, he actually killed a man. He walked away from the charge on a plea of self defense.

One particular Friday evening Pappy had paid everyone and they left except for he and his brother Bill Miller. The two of them had to finish a job of making new wheels for one of the brewery truck wagons that he contracted to keep in operation. After making the wooden spokes and assembling the wheels they would have to bend and fit a metal rim to encircle the wheel which acted like a metal tire. After the circle of metal was welded and driven onto the wooden wheel the outer edge had to be crimped inward to keep it in place. I was in the shop watching them finish this job. I was sitting in the doorway on a stool, looking up the street in front of Lang's Radio Shop when I saw Pee Wee headed toward the front door of the shop. He was staggering and roaring drunk. As he walked into the shop he screamed, "Miller give me my Goddamn money!" Pappy said, "Pee Wee, I have already paid you for this week... now go home and sleep it off"... Pee Wee replied, "Well then give me an advance on next week's pay." Pappy told him, "No." Pee Wee whipped out a knife with a blade which was about six inches long and swung it across Pappy's abdomen literally cutting him open. Pappy stepped back as Pee Wee made a second pass yelling, "I am going to cut your Goddamn guts out!" Pappy grabbed the knife by the blade. It was super sharp and cut deeply into Pappy's left hand between the thumb and first finger. Blood was flying everywhere. Pappy kept backing up until his right hand touched the two by two solid oak board which leaned against the side of one of the forges. Pappy used it to prop things up with. The piece of wood was about thirty inches long. Pappy came up with the board and hit Pee Wee on the right side of his head and then came back from the opposite direction hitting Pee Wee on the left side of his head. Pee Wee stood motionless for a second or two, then charged Pappy again. Pappy came up with the board under Pee Wee's chin and he dropped the knife. Using the board like a baseball bat, Pappy hit him on the right side and then the left. Finally right in the mouth knocking out two teeth. By then the police were there and took both men to the hospital.

About six weeks later Pee Wee showed up at the shop again. Very meekly he said to Pappy, "Mr. Miller, I want to apologize to you. I know I can never make it up to you but I do beg you to forgive me. I have joined the church. I will never take another drink and I want to thank you for beating the hell out of me... otherwise I might be dead." As far as we know he never drank again and, amazingly, Pappy put him back to work for him. Pain and pleasure really is the basis of all learning.

Before I was in my teens Pappy had built a large assortment of magical paraphernalia for me--both smaller stage effects and illusions. We would send away for workshop plans and Pappy would build them. Sometimes Willard would show Pappy how a trick should look and work.

Chapter 7

TWISTS AND TURNS

I think at times when he had no bookings, or some other worry beset him, was when Harry Willard drank the most. He denied it of course. When he was really hitting the "sauce" hard and not eating for several days at a time he would become very depressed and paranoid. Illustratively when his oldest son, Howard, got out of the service he wanted to borrow money, government insured, and rebuild the show to its once magnificent state. Harry went along with it up to a point. Howard had selected new rolling stock (trucks) and was about to order a new theatrical top (tent). Harry blew up and accused Howard of everything vile under the sun. He ran Howard off, and as a result, they did not speak for years.

When his next to youngest daughter Frances, married, Harry accused her of deserting him when he needed her most. He was depending on her taking her mother's place. Frances was simply trying to survive and have a life which she could not have had with Harry. His mental state resulted in a love/hate relationship with virtually everyone with whom he was close. Today Frances is successfully married to a mentalist named Glen Falkenstein and she presents a version of the "Spirit cabinet" act which Joy and Harry literally "killed" audiences with for so many, many years. What

Frances does is not Harry's presentation; it is only a part of it. A strip of cloth is around her neck and each wrist. That cloth is nailed to an upright board mounted to the floor. When the curtain is drawn across the front of the cabinet which conceals her, she extricates herself by cutting the cloth with a hidden razor blade. Various manifestations occur within the cabinet. A volunteer from the audience comes on stage, sits in the cabinet, and holds her wrists to make sure there is no funny business. The curtains are closed. When the curtains are jerked open the volunteer has a bucket over his head and Frances is wearing the coat. Throughout the trick Frances was blindfolded and the audience believed spirits did all of it and not her. When Joy and Harry did the trick near the end, three ghosts came out of the cabinet and started to descend into the audience. The thing that Harry would occasionally do if there were magicians in the audience, and he really wanted to impress them, he would have the volunteer take the coat off and let Harry hold it. After the man was seated in the cabinet holding the mediums wrists, Harry would draw the curtains and do something that was as fast as the vanishing "bird cage act." He would throw the volunteer's coat over the top of the curtain and in the same motion yank the curtain open and Joy would be wearing the coat. He did this entirely too quickly for it to occur. He told me that he rarely did this bit of business but that he would use a "plant" or "stooge" in the audience and he had two coats just alike. One coat was concealed on the outer back of the cabinet, which is never turned around, and all of the stage lights were turned off except for the very bright footlights. This threw a shadow on the backdrop about four feet higher than the cabinet due to the angle at which the lights were pointing. As Harry threw the coat over the curtain he simply threw it a little harder and farther than be generally would so that the coat went on over the cabinet and landed behind it. Someone behind the backdrop would hook the coat and drag it on under the curtain to backstage. In the meanwhile the other coat had been taken down and put on by the medium well before Harry threw the first coat It appeared to be instantaneous.

Harry always wanted to have a lion or tiger to use in an illusion. Virgil Mulkey (Virgil the Magician) gave Harry an ocelot. The damn cat ripped Harry's pants off and chased him up a tree. He never used the animal and got rid of him immediately.

24

I have explained that it made no difference how ill or how intoxicated Harry was, he always gave a flawless performance. I do not think he could have given a bad show even if he tried. When he walked out on the stage everyone really felt as if they were in the presence of royalty. There was only one exception to this that I know of. Harry was really looped and we had all tried to get him to eat something...anything. He refused. (I think we were in Three Rivers at the time). We finally managed to get Willard's full dress suit and his cape on him. Then he did not want to go on. We explained to him that he had a full house and he had to perform. The curtain opened and we pushed him out on the stage whereupon he presented the entire opening of the show perfectly. There was only one thing wrong. Somehow he had gotten turned around and was facing the back curtain and doing the magic for that curtain and not the audience. The crowd could not figure what was happening. At last we turned him around and he went right on with the performance and for some weird reason the audience must have thought it was part of the show and it was their fault they were missing something. Truth is stranger than fiction.

I was playing in Norman, Oklahoma. Delora Whitney, "The magic lady of the south" lived in Norman. She was a great friend of both Harry and mine. Delora came down to the auditorium and said she had a call from Harry's daughter, Madeline, and they had been trying to locate me to see if I could go and find out about Harry because he was very ill and living at a catholic church in Church Point, Louisiana. I called and got very little information. Norman was the last date at the end of a three-month tour. As soon as the show was loaded I sent the truck on to San Antonio and took a station wagon and drove to Church Point. The Father at the church had actually given Harry permission to live in his house car (a refurbished semi-trailer) on the church property. He had hooked up to the church's water and electricity, but had no heat and it was freezing cold. The home on wheels was well equipped with kitchen, two bedrooms, and a bath; but the heat depended on propane and Harry had used all of his money for heat of another kind...alcohol. Harry, his youngest son little Patrick (Emil Patrick Willard), and Frances had actually been living on several bushels of sweet potatoes someone had given them. Harry said he knew more ways to serve sweet potatoes (he called them yams) than anyone else on earth. He had not lost his sense of humor but was coughing every breath, sometimes with blood, and was so emaciated that he was skin and bones. He was literally starving. I took Frances and Pat to a motel; Harry refused to go. I gave him some money and asked what else I could do for him. He said, "Set some spots." I told him that he was in no condition to work. He became furious. He said, "You just get them and let me worry about playing them." I agreed but only if it was alright to work phones. Harry said, "Alright...alright." Later I found out that he really did not understand how telephone promotions operated. I had Carl Balmer come down and both of us went out and booked a string of dates, rented offices, installed the telephones, had tickets, receipts, envelopes, etc. printed for every town. We ordered big billing paper from Neal Walters Showprint in Rogers, Arkansas, had crew managers come in and started selling tickets. I guess I had invested about two thousand dollars in this little tour around Louisiana for Harry. Harry wanted to go with us while we were doing the billing (posting window cards and posters). In one town he went into one of the offices with us where we were selling the advance tickets; it scared him to death. Never, even in his hey day, had he seen anyone sell so many tickets so fast and collectors go out and pick up the money. He had in his mind that someone was stealing all of this money. He did not understand that the telephone solicitors had to be paid on a daily basis. He went to every town and told the sponsor that there was a bunch of crooks booking his show and selling tickets and stealing all the money. He was drunk as a skunk when he did this, but they believed him simply because he had an established reputation in every town in Louisiana. I explained the truth of the matter to them and they seemed to understand but I insisted that each sponsor take over its own promotion because I did not think that a joint enterprise could flourish in an atmosphere of distrust. I turned all of the printed material over to the sponsors. Harry did not want me to do that; he wanted me to turn it over to him. I made each sponsor sign a release stating that I would no longer be responsible. I thank heaven that we had not commenced the campaigns in all the towns. (Probably only about eight or ten of them). I had to pay everyone off and took one heck of a beating. I had booked Harry and promoted him many times before, but had never used phones. Within two months he was calling

26

me for money and wanting me to get him some more dates. NEVER AGAIN!

I took little Pat to Howard in Deer Park, Texas, and Frances to San Antonio. Little Gloria Ann (Harry's youngest daughter) was living with Doc and Anne Sterling (Mahendra). Finally little Gloria Ann was adopted by a family named Dornaby and she later moved to Alaska. Tragedy struck shortly after I took Pat to Howard. The little fellow was out riding his bicycle when he was struck by a vehicle and killed. I have always regretted taking Pat to Howard. Had I left him in Louisiana with his father, he might still be alive. I am sorry Pat.

Chapter 8

SOME SECRETS

Harry Willard always had a real thing about wanting to "cut down the margins" on his illusions. No matter how small an effect might be he thought he could make it smaller...he frequently did. I think that was because he was such a small man. He was tiny and very dapper. The "Girl without a middle" illusion is one wherein an upright cabinet which has five doors opening down the front. A door for each leg, two middle doors and one at the top where the assistants head is located. In performance a lady is placed inside the cabinet with shackles around her wrists, knees, and throat. Two large blades which are the width of the cabinet are forced through at the neck level and just above the knees. The lower doors are opened and the audience can see her knees and legs on down to the bottom. The top door is opened and viewers may see her head. Both legs and head move to prove that it is a live girl, but when the two center doors are opened the torso part of her body from the neck down to just above the knees is gone. To disprove any chicanery the magician walks around to the back and opens, backward, a back door and the audience can plainly see through the whole thing. The lady's middle really is G-O-N-E.

What really happens is that the back door of the cabinet, in most models, have two doors that open inward but when closed and locked can be opened outward and back as a single door. Once the young lady is in the cabinet, she has a place to sit down with her rear end sticking out of the backside and she closes the two back doors in front of her. It is her real legs which are seen by the audience and the head is a fake but a good duplicate of her--identical makeup, wig, etc., make this possible. Well, most models of the trick have a least one failing. If an audience is too close they can see the separation in the back door. Harry changed all of that--he constructed a back door that operated like an old-fashioned roll top desk. The back rolled up over the girls head when she would bend over in the cabinet. He glued some material over the part that rolled up and painted it to match the rest of the cabinet. Regardless of how close a person was, it nevertheless looked as though the back door was solid. *(See Appendix B-3)*

One night Harry came in smashed and decided the cabinet was too wide so he took a saw and proceeded to cut six inches off making it entirely too small for any woman to get into. He ruined a wonderful version of one of the world's greatest illusions. It made no difference that he had other versions of the same trick.

Harry had seven children named Howard, Rosemary, Eugene, Madeline, Frances, Gloria, and Pat. (Howard being the oldest and they are in descending order). When Rosemary was young she was lithe of figure. She did not tolerate food or alcohol very well. Unlike Harry she started to gain weight early on.

Harry had the most wonderful of glass lined trunks. *(See Appendix B-4)* Much different from commercial models. If he really wanted to, he could have the girl appear instantly visible and without any covering of the trunk. Harry had cut it down and cut it down-- always trying to make it smaller. Rosemary kept getting bigger. Harry took the trick back off and installed springs he had gotten from an old Ford automobile with 50 times the tension of the original. As the girl appears there is an instant when she is being balanced, precariously, on a very small ledge and the second back door (the presence of which is unknown to the onlookers) literally propel the woman into the inside of the lighted trunk. Harry's wife, Joy, had always done it. Rosemary did not know about the new springs--or if she did know, was looped and forgot. Harry had broken the thick front sheet of glass that is between the girl and the audience and he had replaced that sheet of glass (counter glass) with thin, cheap window pane glass. The gun was fired and Rosemary appeared alright. She came flying through that thing like a shot, right on through the pane glass and out onto the stage and finally landed in the orchestra pit. All Harry could say was, "Boy, she's quite an arm full, isn't she?" Poor Rosemary was all cut up, the glass was ruined and Harry would end up replacing the glass with the sturdier, thicker variety.

Chapter 9

STILL MORE SECRETS, ETC.

Appearances in houses and auditoriums mandated modifications in the Willard programs because so many of the "miracles" which he accomplished were a direct result of what went on beneath "his" stage. Several levitations operated from under the stage--many productions, instant transformations, vanishes and much, which today, magicians can only dream about.

The "Duck tub" was an illusion of which a big, wooden wash tub was shown empty. The inside was painted flat black and therefore the audience could not see the revolving disk (the inside diameter of the tub) which hid four separate compartments each of which contained, out of sight, a live white duck. The tub sat on a pedestal and buckets of water were poured into the tub until it was full. Each bucket had a letter of the alphabet painted on the front if it. When the buckets were lined up the letters spelled out "W-I-L-L-A-R-D the W-I-Z-A-R-D." Harry would magically produce four eggs. One at a time he would toss the eggs onto the surface of the water whereupon it looked as though it immediately burst into a live duck flapping its wings. It all took place because some poor fellow under the stage reached up into the tub's mechanisms and turned the disk with a special rod-type tool. To avoid water running down onto him was an impossibility so, consequently, that person got a bath nightly whether he needed it or not.

One of the most beautiful, startling, and confounding mysteries presented by Willard was his inexhaustible bottle. He took a large champagne bottle and set it down on a side table. He would ask members of the audience to call out the names of preferred colors. Each time a different color was mentioned he took a little hook and reached into the mouth of the bottle and pulled out a long, beautiful ribbon of that color. After this went on for a while, it became perfectly obvious that, in bulk alone, there seemed to be much more than could ever fit back into that bottle. If someone called out an exotic combination of colors he would, nevertheless, pull it out. Very profound stuff. The large array of colored ribbons was concealed on a rack made for easy access, under the stage. With an extension the person under the stage would take the ribbon called for and shove it up through the floor, and the leg of the side stand table, and into the bottom of the bottle. That bottle was specially turned out of heavy steel and could only be lifted with some difficulty. The bottle was painted black. When an unusual, or exotic, color needed to be produced Willard had a "plant" placed out in the audience with instructions to call out that particular item. Worked very well.

Chapter 10

TRICKS AND MORE TRICKS

Willard liked to do a trick with a glass case that was approximately 12" by 12" by 18" and it did have a top. The case could be seen through at virtually any angle. This case was filled with red and dark blue balls. He would take a couple of the balls out and bounce them to demonstrate their authenticity. He would remove all the balls from the glass case, place them in another box of equal size, fire a revolver, show the second container empty, and the glass case immediately re-filled itself with the balls. Willard had enough different effects to fill a small encyclopedia.

Willard had a canary in the light bulb. I know the history of this particular mystery and it is an interesting one. It was, definitively the very best version of this trick. "Birch the Magician" made a reputation with the trick but it was nowhere nearly as effective as the one I am going to explain. Sitting on a side table, on stage, was a thin chrome stand. Much like the stand for a P&L clock vanish. The upright rod was about 1/2" in diameter. On the top of this rod, about 14" above the table top was seen burning a clear (not frosted) 100 watt bare light bulb. There was nothing else within many feet of the burning bulb. An assistant brought out a cage containing a live canary. The bird was removed from the cage, placed inside a small paper sack (the neck of the sack was bunched up), and Willard would fire a revolver at the sack. The explosion of the gun literally blew the bag into many pieces and the canary was gone. At the same instant the gun was fired, the light bulb went out and seen inside of that bulb, squirming around, was the live canary. Willard would take the hot bulb down into the audience and allow members to touch the bulb and look, very closely, at the live bird inside. The bulb was then broken, inside of the cage, and the bird fluttered out. I have seen just about all the others, especially the one that is covered with a lampshade until the time for the bulb to go out and the bird reappear, and none of them even start to compare with this version. Bill Copeland, Madeline (Willard) Copeland's husband, still has that piece of equipment today.

When Willard did the "rat bottle" trick and after the bottle was broken open to allow the bunny, rat, dove or whatever, to be taken from the broken bottle with the borrowed rings or wrist watch tied around the animal's neck, Willard would take a little hammer and break the bottle up into many little pieces proving it was not the conventional metal shell bottle. *(See Appendix B-5)*

I guess another book based solely upon Willard's special tricks, or his unique adaptations of others, should be written. Willard's presentations convinced audiences that they were seeing "real magic."

I remember his peculiar boiler tank escape. This brain buster was a tank that was about 3 1/2' high and approximately 30" in diameter. This tank was made of genuine steel boiler plating and the seams were welded together. The tank had a lid, made of the same material that completely covered the top of the tank and a lid lip that extended down the side of the tank about three inches. Two large holes, each about 3/4" in diameter, were drilled through the lip of the lid and through the tank proper. These holes allowed for a steel rod, or bar, to slide through so when the lid was on the tank and the holes lined up the bar could slide through the holes and a padlock was attached to each end. This made the removal of the bar impossible and the tank's lid equally so. A committee from the audience would come on stage and thoroughly examine the tank which was filled to the very top with water. A power hose accomplished this in a relatively short period of time. When the tank was full of water Willard would climb into the tank dispersing an amount of water equal to his size and weight. This was always the last trick in that particular

34

show because water went all over hell and back and Willard was, of course, soaked. There being little or no air space when the lid was in place made staying in there for very long an exceedingly hazardous proposition. All the time the tank was being filled with water, the steel rod was being passed around in the audience. In the advertisement, audience members were challenged to bring their own padlocks in order to secure the lid. After Willard was submerged in the water and the lid locked in place on the tank, two local welders would proceed to "spot" weld the lid in place. The tank had a screen placed in front of it for an instant. The screen was removed but the lid remained intact. The welders cut their welds loose and the padlocks were unlocked and removed together with the rod. The lid was removed and a voice from the back of the theatre cried out "do not do that!"...it was Willard walking down the aisle and his clothing was DRY.

One night in Oklahoma the welders were careless and their welding cables were laying on stage as Willard stepped into the tank. The water overflowed onto the stage and the cables. There was a scream and the electricity sent Willard flying through the air into his own orchestra pit--very lively performance that night.

The reason Willard could do the "dancing hank" in such bright light was his thread drop. He told me that it took his family about 10 years to produce that curtain. As I recall the basic material was dark grey but there were, quite literally, thousands of embroidery threads, of every color and variation of color, one at a time, sewn through the curtain and tied leaving a double tassel to hang down about one to one and a half inches. This myriad of color so confused the eye as to make it impossible to see the "gimmick" threads and wires; and, the brightness of the stage made it all the more perplexing. This was the basis for a great number of Willard's most popular items.

When Willard did the vanishing bird cage he did not hold the cage down at waist level as did Blackstone and Allerton. Willard held the cage up in front of his face and was looking through it, at the audience, when it instantly, visibly vanished. Harry also had a vanishing bird cage that was round and not rectangular. *(See Appendix B-2)*

In an attempt to define the persona of Harry Willard, I would have to say that he was truly two personalities. Not a paraphrenic, as in the classical, clinical sense, but rather, two people each knowing completely the thoughts and actions of the other. However, neither was knowingly contrived but more natural and simplistic. It all seemed so matter-of-fact. Willard loved to take off his full dress suit and put on his khaki clothing. He really loved to wear his old brown felt fedora with its perspiration soaked hatband. After donning this apparel and taking off his makeup with its moustache and goatee, an unknowing person would never realize that this old man was, in reality, Willard the Wizard. For, Willard, you see, was gregarious, majestic, charismatic, commanding with a powerful voice that truly hypnotized. The old man in khaki was shy, withdrawn, quiet, soft spoken, moody, but very thoughtful.

Frequently when on stage, Willard came to the part of his "patter" that required his mentioning the country of Pakistan, he would purposely substitute the word "khaki-stan" as he looked off stage with a twinkle in his eye and a wink. It was sort of an "in" thing which he did to introduce an "aside" into his subject matter--which was usually composed of a Willardism or a purposeful mispronunciation or malaprop. These little things added to his charm, which simply, could not be resisted.

Wearing one of the "black men" suits (all flat black including a hood) while working marionettes allowed the tiny doll characters to seem so lifelike that they really did have personalities of their own. All of the Willards were super marionette manipulators. I only saw Tommy and Harry, but young as I was, I felt that Harry did it the very best. He made his audience want to go down and shake hands with (and talk to) the little figures. Harry was great at carving the puppets. He did it all including making their clothing, painting them, and stringing. Terrific!

Harry gave me a really beautiful antique looking, loaded with gingerbread, black velvet screen that was about three feet high and two feet wide. It looked like a coat-of-arms and stood on a stand. This screen had a small, clear light bulb that was mounted at the very top. This was what Harry called a "manipulation screen" because it had traps that were, of course, concealed. They tilted back and forth and had black velvet covered whale bone openings the size of two-inch billiard balls (but which were so carefully hidden that spectators would never know of their existence) and various other "hook," "pins," and "gimmicks" that would allow a truly remarkable display of manipulative skill even if the demonstrator was not so gifted.

Chapter 11

WILLARD AND
WOMEN'S UNDERPANTS...

Once my asthma was under control, thanks to a Mr. Myers who brought me the first nebulizer and adrenaline solution for inhalation in our area, and perhaps the entire city, I started to gain weight. I was always rather tall for my age and quickly developed an older appearance. Most of the time I passed for an advancement in my age of several years. I seem to have always spoken like an older person. In my teens this enabled me to go into the establishments specializing in libations. Proprietors either thought I was older or Willard and/or my grandfather would introduce me as a son or grandson. This seemed to cover the matter pretty well, but I also think, that most of those operating taverns did not really care back in those days. They were only interested in selling booze. I must confess that I had developed an interest in drinking it.

I would take off from school to go on camp shows and to tag along with the Willard show. This happened with ever increasing frequency. The Catholic school which I attended made allowances for my absences. The "Brothers (and fathers) of Mary Order" ran the school. I did fund raising performances for them and they seemed to

38

appreciate the money so much that I, and a fellow named Marlin "Corky" Plunkett were in the rather unique position of having our "truancies" winked at. This went well until a change of administration came along. One thing we were compelled to do was to keep our "assignments" up to date and phone in almost daily. The brothers would often move on over to St. Mary's University. Most all of the brothers and fathers were completely capable of teaching at both the high school and college levels and most had more degrees than a thermometer. The Brothers of Mary also operated St. Mary's University except for the law school which was downtown.

Some of the Brothers and Fathers did teach law--not all of them. Later the Law School, under the direction of Dean Ernest Raba, moved out to the University campus. Thank God for Brother Norman Kramer and some of the others, or else all would be lost insofar as my smattering of education is concerned.

I remember that one time while in Louisiana with the Willard entourage Harry discovered a perplexing problem. The folding chairs for the show would have fresh, clean chair covers on their backs every third night. One night they would all be red, then three days later they would be blue, and finally following another third day they would be white. Willard started noticing large numbers of the chair covers missing after the show. Many times--as many as 30 or more. They would be replaced after Harry would buy the material and the ladies on the show would cut and sew them. Still it was a bother and quite an expense in both time and money. After this went on long enough Harry started making inquires into what could possibly be behind such a nuisance. Finally, one night after the performance he saw the tail end of a red chair cover sticking out from under a lady's coat. He did not say anything but started rushing up to the front following the show in order to simply watch. After one matinee he collared the man with one of the women that he knew had taken a chair cover. Willard asked the man why the covers were being taken. After all if someone just wanted a souvenir there were plenty of others available. The man said, "Mr. Willard don't you know that you have put underpants on half the women in Louisiana??" They stole the chaircovers and cut the two corners out of them, turned them upside down, put some elastic or a safety pin and a new pair of panties was created.

I mentioned Corky Plunkett who was out on the road as the

39

star performer of "Dailey Brothers Circus," Corkey held the world's record on a trampoline and could bounce all of the way to the top of the tent 143 times doing a triple somersault in the process. Corky and his whole family traveled with the circus in one capacity or another. There really were no Dailey Brothers that was just a name for the circus. It was owned and operated by Ben Davenport with Winter Quarters in Gonzales, Texas. Davenport was a great friend and admirer of Harry Willard. Rumors were abound that that circus was the toughest show that ever hit America...bar none. When a patron came onto the circus lot both a "dip mob" (pickpockets) and a "broad mob" (three card monte swindlers) would grab them. Very often, before the potential customer got to the box office to buy tickets, all of his money and wallet were simply GONE.

While the customers were in the circus "prowl mobs" were out going through the parked cars, stealing what they could, and siphoning the gasoline out of the tanks. That show never bought the first nickel's worth of gasoline to move the trucks and tractors.

The show traveled by rail and had its own train including sleeping cars. They carried an extra boxcar to throw in what was stolen each day. Even things like motor scooters, lawn chairs, roller skates...whatever was not tied down was vulnerable. Each season the show found itself with less and less bookings because "Dailey Brothers" bad reputation preceded it. That circus had what was known as the "pie car" on the train where, after the men were paid their salaries, there was drinking and gambling. Professional gamblers in that "pie car" were there for the sole purpose of taking the employees' money back from them. I do not know why they did not simply strong arm them because those poor people just did not have any chance of winning.

In addition, the story was that Davenport caught his wife in bed with his bookkeeper; he acted as if it did not matter. Shortly after that discovery, the bookkeeper's body was found in the "elephant car" where the shifting weight of the elephants crushed him to death while enroute between cities. Only time in history that the entire trainload of circus employees were arrested. That is, all except one who was a pregnant lady about to deliver.

Later to keep his wife from profiting in any way from the enterprise, Davenport purposely bankrupted the circus and left the

40

three sections of the train standing on a siding. Davenport took a gigantic python and a boa constrictor to Alaska. They had never seen live snakes in Alaska. One of the snakes died. Ben reduced the price of admission from $10 to $5. People lined up for blocks to walk through and see these reptiles in huge glass cages. Finally the other snake died. Davenport went right on exhibiting the dead snake until the stench was so bad that no one could go near it. Then Davenport died. The world is probably better off.

Chapter 12

THE NET AND OTHER NONSENSE

The "Dizzy Limit" illusion is one which most illusionists have included in their programs. "Birch" used it to vanish Princess, his miniature Shetland pony; "Virgil" used it to vanish "Julie;" and Blackstone, Sr. used it to vanish three girls on a swing. The basic principle is relatively simple. A large rope net is hanging in a frame and a hammock, swing or something to support the person, animal or item that is to be vanished, hangs in front. The net is brought around, under, and finally, up in front of the vanishee. It is attached at about the same height in both front and back. In other words the "vanishee" is encased in the net. A gun is fired, a puff of smoke escapes, and the "vanishee" is gone. Actually, there are two nets--one is hanging slightly in front of the one the audience sees but is out of sight and the audience never knows it exists. On the backside of the front net is a piece of cloth that matches the backdrop so the audience thinks they are seeing through the net to the back curtain. The blank gun is fired and the puff of smoke goes up just as the hidden net drops down. To the spectators it looks as though the "vanishee" went up in a puff of smoke. In reality the "vanishee" remains exactly in the same position as he started. There is a duplicate swing, hammock, or support which drops down with the duplicate net and background. *(See Appendix B-*

6)

Willard liked mine because it had a unique device for tripping the drop of the second net. I told him that he could borrow it to copy or he could make plans for a later use but that I was not going to give it to him. I needed it and I knew what he wanted to do with it. He intended "cutting down the margins" and using it to vanish a dog.

The way we had it rigged up, the frame containing the net was painted flat black and masked by two palm trees bending toward each other. We had some flat set pieces like a pyramid sitting on stage also. The girl that vanished wore a sarong which had a top to cover her chest and a skirt of the same material. It was just a rectangular cloth and it was wrapped around her middle and tied in a knot on the left side above the hip. This let the skirt hang half open and sort of show her left leg. When the girl put it on she would pull her panties up from below and down from above and tie them with a piece of ribbon, otherwise the panties would show. On this terrible occasion, the girl was not wearing briefs but the longer leg panties and she could find nothing to tie them. She felt safe in simply leaving them off thinking no one could see since she was in a lying position all the while and was reclined when the curtain opened for the trick. Well two things happened that had never happened before and never happened again. The front net was set just a little too close to the back one and the weight that made it fall very fast hit the girl just enough to throw her off balance. Her weight tore the back net down as she was falling to the floor but the sarong got hung on some sort of a protrusion on the back side of the very narrow board on which she had been laying. I think that it was a nail or screw that had not been driven in all the way. To make the story as short as possible it literally ripped the sarong off of her and she landed, buck naked from the waist down, amid the ropes of the net. The shock almost brought the law for an indecent exposure charge. I gave the damn trick to Willard.

Aside from familial ties Willard had another affinity for Louisiana. It was possible to purchase liquor by the drink in the Cajun state. Prohibition continued in many areas of Texas long after the repeal of the Volstead Act. As a matter of fact a lot of people made money smuggling alcoholic beverages into those dry areas. For that reason Willard had to acquaint himself with bootleggers in virtually every dry area.

While San Antonio was no longer "dry" it was just simply impossible to purchase "booze" there on a Sunday. I remember the Willard show was set up on the grounds of the Catholic church (I think that it was St. Henry's) near Nogalitos and South Flores Streets. I was over there and Harry was showing me some different "moves" with the Billiard Balls trick. He used a burning candle for this and it looked (to the audience) like he kept pulling balls out of the flame. It suddenly hit him that he had failed to "stock up" on his favorite fuel the day before; so he handed me a $10 bill along with a hastily scribbled note and gave me instructions to a nearby Chinese groceryman. I got on my bicycle and rode over there. The store was closed but when I went around to the back door and knocked, the man came and took the note and money. He said, "You wait," and a few minutes later he returned with a fifth of whiskey and a fifth of gin. The Willard show was in business for another day. I certainly would not want it to sound as though Harry, or his wife, were non-functional without the alcohol but it was near it. Willard was either equal to or darn near the temperament and moods of those which I have read about the great W.C. Fields but much more agile, better looking, and a much crisper, powerful, distinct manner of speech.

Chapter 13

OTHER MAGICAL ENTERTAINERS
I HAVE KNOWN

Through Willard, Dittmar, and Frank Sterling (the Great Mahendra) I was introduced to, and became friends of, most of the great magicians of the time.

I met McDonald Birch (Birch the Magician) through Willard. Birch and his wife Mabel (Mabel Sperry) lived in Ohio but traveled the entire nation with a gigantic show for over 40 years. They featured, "Princess the vanishing pony." That was the meanest little Shetland pony that ever lived. She would bite hell out of anyone. Mac and Mabel were married in Laredo, Texas, so whenever they played San Antonio they would leave their huge semi show trucks at our house and take a nostalgic trip to Laredo. Mac was a handsome devil and one of the better magicians presenting a full evening show. Mabel played the marimba very well. The only thing lacking was in Birch's voice. He did not have the powerful, distinct, commanding voice of Willard, Calvert, or Blackstone.

John Dittmar played a heavy role in my collection of magical props and knowledge. Dittmar the Magician had been a global traveler. By formal training he was an engineer. He was a part of a royal family in Germany. At one time he owned one of the largest magical manufacturing companies in the world and it was located in Hamburg, Germany. He had fabulous wealth. He built the first truly high rise apartments in San Antonio. It was a splendid structure which, in its museum like lobby, exhibited works of art that were rumored to be worth several million dollars. John Dittmar is mentioned in the book, "Illustrated Magic by Ottokar Fischer" as being the only white man ever to actually see a version of the fabled Hindu Rope trick in India. He explained the secret working of that miracle to me. *(See Appendix A-4)*

It was through John Dittmar that I met Joseffy. His real name was Josef Freud. Joe Freud had one of the most brilliant scientific minds to ever grace magic and the world generally. He invented the Johansen Blocks. These are the instruments used in ultra fine machine work for the micro measuring into the thousandths of an inch.

Joseffy had a trick known as the "Expanding trunk." He would show the audience a miniature trunk. Visibly, in his hands, the trunk would enlarge to four times its size. While watching, spectators would gasp as it enlarged a second time to eight times its original size. Turning around he would sit the trunk on a little platform and as he stepped away, the audience would see that, now, it had grown to the proportions normally associated with a regular trunk whereupon the lid would open and out would step his assistant. One can assume that the assistant was concealed in the platform prior to appearance but the mechanics allowing for the expansion of the trunk were a real brain buster.

Joseffy loved to demonstrate his fantastic "Skull of Balsamo." This was a real skull which he would take from its carrying case and Joseffy would take his pocket handkerchief and wipe the top of the skull saying that "this is the actual skull of Count Balsamo." Then looking down he would say, "as you can plainly see the Count was a polished gentleman." He proceeded to place the skull on top of the sheet of glass that was resting between two chairs. Any place to which he would walk in the auditorium, that skull would turn and look at him. Questions asked from the audience would be answered by the skull clicking its teeth together... once for yes and twice for no.

John Dittmar and his brother, Guido, lived in the family home which was next door to the Aurora Apartments built by John. They had such a "falling out" that they actually had a partition built right down the center of the mansion so that neither of them would have to see the other.

Before his death John married. I think his wife's name was Thera. One day Guido showed up at our home with several trailers full of magic and furnishings. It even included the family album.. He asked my mother if he could leave it all in one of our garages. Later, after years passed, he called and left word that if there was anything there that we wanted, to consider it ours; we never heard from him again. In that stuff was a tremendous amount of magic. I suppose he did not want John's widow to have it.

Dittmar was a great friend of the well-known South American magician "Fu Manchu." Fu's real name was David Bamberg and he corresponded with John Dittmar on a regular basis. Then, without explanation it stopped. Later I heard that because John Dittmar was accused of being a Nazi Bamberg, with close family members still living in Germany, and Jewish, did not want to have any further communications with Dittmar. I understand that the FBI investigated Dittmar but nothing ever came of it.

Chapter 14

INTERESTING WILLARDISMS

Harry Willard had an absolute abhorrence of business matters particularly as they pertained to money. He was the true artist and held financial matter in great disdain. Harry was a perfectionist but he always sought to be "more than perfect." Everyone that ever saw him would agree that he always gave a flawless performance, yet somehow, Harry always truly believed that it could be better and that such art should not have to be influenced by financial strain. He was keenly aware of his inadequacies in finance and bookkeeping. This led to a problem with the Internal Revenue Service which was just about as bad as it can get. They filed on him for non-payment of several taxes including, but not limited to, withholding. He was so ill that he really could not stand up and the tax agents attached (confiscated) the show. Since Harry had, if you will remember, at least two other shows it was irrelevant in so far as he was concerned. When his health improved he was back in business. He was plagued with the ups and downs of his physical problems most of his life.

Willard, due to dereliction of his duties in business, had a terrible fear of the day when his father would retire and turn the show over to him. He loved the performing but would actually break out in a "cold sweat" at the thought of contracting, bookkeeping, bill paying, etc... so he ran off. He joined Christy Brothers Circus. George Christy was a great friend of both Harry and his father.

Harry was self taught when it came to wire walking, juggling, and believe it or not, working as a trapeze artist. He could do all those things, and from what I have heard, he did them well; but, I know that he did them as acts of desperation in order to try an escape which he knew to be inevitable... the day that he would have to pick up the mantle of WILLARD THE WIZARD.

Willard's father died. I think that it was about 1936 or 1937. A few months later, his brother, Tommy, was killed in the train accident. Overnight the new Willard the Wizard ascended the throne. He did it great credit.

Under Harry's guidance the show thrived greater than ever before; but, though he denied it, that very success took its toll on him. He now had this reputation which he had to continually justify. Wherever he was found, he was entertaining someone with sleight of hand. I guess everyone had seen many of the stunts which he performed but never--and I do mean N-E-V-E-R--were they done as Harry did them. The commonest of tricks in his hands seemed entirely different somehow. Let me illustrate... the Linking Ring mystery is a trick in which the magician seemingly causes silver rings of eight, ten, or twelve inch diameters to magically link themselves together. The metal really looked like it was melting through itself and, in the end, all eight rings would be linked together in a chain which Harry would, slowly separate, one at a time, and toss them to members of the audience to inspect.

The Billiard Ball trick in which two-inch billiard balls magically appeared, disappeared, and multiplied at his fingertips became all the more convincing when he dropped both hands down in front of him and slowly turned his hands, back and forth, showing the front and back of each hand to be empty even though, in truth, each contained a ball.

Harry did all of the tricks using invisible thread. Floating ball, light bulb, glass of milk, skull, dancing handkerchief, etc... when necessary he could do each such mystery by himself... without the aid of assistants.

Harry did Thurston's "Rising Cards" mystery, using five cards, masterfully. For the "Rising and Floating Cards," as Harry called it, he did not use a "reel" (a device well known to magicians) and he did perform this trick without the benefit of any kind of helpers. *(See Appendix B-7)*

One time Harry and brother Tommy decided to try and earn some "pin" money above and beyond their weekly allowance. They were very small children, still, they were able to talk a local property owner into letting them use the front end of one of his unoccupied store buildings on the main street of the town. They cut the paper dolls out of grocery sacks and Harry got up in the window while Tommy stood off to the side. Tommy acted totally disinterested and pretended to be reading a comic book while Harry stood the dolls up and made them dance. Tommy was working the "gimmick." No one seemed to notice Tommy. Passersby would marvel at the "dancing dolls." They were selling like "hot cakes" at ten cents each. All went well until Harry's father, Jim Willard, came walking down the street and saw what was going on. Jim came roaring in and all hell broke loose. After giving the boys the thrashing of a lifetime he said, "do you not realize that you are exposing one of the most profound illusions on our show?" That put an end to the doll company.

Harry did the "card star." This is a trick that magic companies used to sell. It was approximately 14" across. The magician would go into the audience with a deck of cards and have five of the cards freely selected. He would vanish the cards; then miraculously and instantly, the cards reappeared with one projecting from the end of each point of the five-pointed star. This was accomplished by forcing the cards on the spectators. Duplicates of those cards were on the back of the apparatus and, at the proper time, would be jerked out to the point of the star by a rubber band-type device on the back . Anyone looking at the back of it would immediately know how and where the cards were concealed and what made them reappear.

Harry's card star was different. One thing he did was to have the cards selected from the deck after giving that deck to a member of the audience. In other words he was not holding the deck when the cards were chosen. He would then give each person that had taken a card, a pen or pencil and ask them to write their names on the face of that card. He would walk back on stage to a pretty, shiny metal stand with a round silver disk attached to a center rod. From this disk ran five other rods, each sticking out at a different angle, and about, one

50

half inch (or less) in diameter. Harry would throw the deck at the star and each of the five selected cards would appear at the end of one of the tiny rods. The cards were each given back to the selector as a souvenir after that person did authenticate the fact that it was their same card. Whereupon Harry would disassemble the "star" and slowly show both sides of each and every piece demonstrating it to be free and clear of chicanery.

I think that the only time my grandmother came really close to leaving my grandfather was the time that he disappeared for several days (rumor had it as a week and some even said longer). What happened was that Willard came into San Antonio after being along the border in Del Rio, Eagle Pass, Laredo, and other towns playing shows. He had been on the road for quite a while and accumulated a good deal of money. As a mater of fact Harry was loaded... in more ways than one. He came and picked up my grandfather and the two of them went to the old "Gleam Bar" on Dolorosa Street. They had the owner, a friend of both men, lock the doors and they bought round after round of food and drink. They were there for so long that Harry and Charley were both reported missing. When my grandfather finally made it home he was not feeling very well. I can remember my grandmother yelling, "You old fool...if you do not have any better sense than to do something like this you can just go on and die." I thought that was a simply terrible thing to say to a sick man. He was sick--with one of the worst hangovers ever. Mary, my grandmother, said, "Charley, you are going to keep on with that old devil of a Willard until it gets the both of you killed!"... IT NEVER DID.

Harry and Pappy did not believe in womanizing. They made up for it in drinking and sometimes gambling just a little. It was hard for anyone to be convinced that Harry would not "pull some of his tricks" if they gambled with him. So, if and when, he took a chance on a turn of a card or a roll of the dice, it generally had to be with someone that knew nothing of him... they were few.

There was a trick that John Dittmar had which later turned up in Harry's stuff and I wound up with it. It was a forerunner of the "Girl in the Drum." It was different from the others. Sitting on a silver table was what looked like an old-fashioned radio but of giant proportions. Where the speaker would be was open all the way through and could be covered with sheets of paper and metal rings to

51

hold the paper in place. Down where the control knobs were there were disks that could be removed allowing the spectators to see all of the way through just as with the very large hole up above. After demonstrating the entire affair to be empty, the magician would break through the paper and pull out all kinds of objects and livestock such as ducks, rabbits, chicken, silks, umbrellas, etc... finally a lady burst through the paper. No part of this apparatus appeared to be thick enough to conceal the livestock much less the lady. Nevertheless, that is exactly what happened. *(See Appendix B-8)*

Chapter 15

ODDS AND ENDS

Many dictums handed down to me by Willard stuck. To this very day they run through my mind....... One unwritten law was that the show should never pass up a town. If there was no sponsor available then it should be booked and billed as a "still" date. Naturally, it was not always possible. For instance, Plainview, Texas, was a non-playable town. They had a local law against magic shows. Plainview being in the middle of the "Bible Belt" had its share of religious fanatics. I am reasonably religious but these people carried the whole thing to the point of "detachment from reality," which is one of the classic definitions of psychosis (some say insanity).

As late as the last time our show appeared in Cassville, Missouri, religious zealots came down to the auditorium and locked arms in front of the entrance and refused patrons admission. The sheriff had to come and physically remove them. Then they all went across the street to the park and got down on their knees and prayed for our "souls" throughout the performance. *(See Appendix A-5)*

Willard's "law" was applied to the spook shows. Amazingly the big theatre chains actually allowed us to "hop scotch" on the tour. To illustrate, we would play a town for Fox theatres today; and tomorrow in the next town, be owned by Commonwealth Theatres;

and the next town would be an independent. Then the next spot would be operated by Paramount. Then back onto Fox for the next three towns and so on. The chain which we started out on and which was generally the largest would actually arrange with the other theatre operators for our dates in the towns along the way. In other words, the chain really did our booking for us, saving us time and money as well as keeping the appearances relatively close.

In Harry's "cookhouses," which was really a traveling restaurant, there was just about every conceivable pot, pan, cookware, and utility. Harry often did the cooking himself. Obviously, the ability to cook for large numbers of people is much different than what goes on in most kitchens at home. Harry would buy supplies such as flour in 50 pound sacks. When "Willard Stew" was served passersby would stop and ask what that delicious aroma represented and they would try to buy some. Even today that recipe is sought after. When the batter for pancakes was made, it was done in a huge "crock;" and as the men and women came to eat, their pancakes were cooked and served hot on the spot.

If you recall, I had mentioned J.W. "Jimmie" Richardson, a mortician and embalmer, from Fort Worth, Texas. Richardson came to work on my spook show as a booking agent. I first met Richardson while he was supposed to be working as a "twenty-four-hour man" for Willard. The twenty-four-hour man was the person who went ahead of the show and made sure all of the posters were prominently displayed, news stories were "planted" in the newspapers (and sometimes pictures), advertising was purchased, and radio spots were covered. Richardson never made it out ahead of the show because he was always too busy eating. He was almost as big around as he was tall. Willard once said that Richardson had eaten as much as the other 37 people working on the show. Willard did not care how much the man ate, but deeply cared about the fact that he would not go out and work afterward. Harry fired him. On one particular morning there was about half of the crock of pancake mix left and Richardson remained at the stove in the cookhouse frying and eating pancakes until it was all gone. Harry said that he lost count when the man reached the unforgettable number of 34 flapjacks.

One of the big old black frying pans in Willard's cookhouses was, by far, the largest I had ever seen. One day I asked Harry why he needed such a large skillet and he said, "that is what I use to cook my sand in." I thought that he was just teasing me. Later I found out that was exactly what he did. One of his best tricks was his "magic sand." He had a very large fish bowl sitting on a side table on the stage and there were three big canisters sitting beside the bowl. Willard would reach into each canister to grab a handful of sand and let it slowly trickle from between his fingers back into the container. Each of the three canisters contained a different colored sand--one was yellow, one blue, and the other one was red. Then he would take a fist full of sand and drop it into the fishbowl full of water. The water had sort of a cloudy appearance. After a large amount of each colored sand was placed in the bowl of water, Willard would stir the whole mess. When he finished, he would reach into the water and grab a handful of something. When he brought his hand out and held if over the canister, the sand of that color would slowly trickle out again back into that colored sand canister. How did each color remain together and how did it stay dry? That is where the frying pan came in. He would fill the frying pan with oh, let's say, red sand, add chunks of beeswax, and keep stirring the sand over flames until all of the beeswax had melted and each grain of sand was coated. When the sand cooled, a handful could be dribbled out of the hand in singular grains; but, when that same handful was squeezed together, the wax caused the fistful to cling together in a clump that could actually be stirred around in the water and not separate.

Willard loved the "Goddess and the Reptile" illusion. This was a table about three feet square with a drawer in the front. Sitting on the top of the table was an octagon-shaped drum. The drum had a front door that, when opened, allowed a complete view of the entire interior of the drum which was illuminated by eight small light bulbs. About six feet above this affair was a canopy which could be raised or lowered. *(See Appendix B-9)* As with most magical stage properties it was a godawful looking thing. I think that most of the magical equipment defies description. Audiences immediately know what it is because of the phoniness of its appearance and the paint jobs which, usually, insults the eye. If magicians "stage furniture" looked more like what it is intended to be, the presentations would be all the more powerful.

In the Willard presentation of the "Goddess and the Reptile" a rectangular flower box overflowing with beautiful flowers was put on top of the drum. A slate was attached to the backside of the flower box in an upright position. Slowly, from up out of the flowers, came a green snake with a piece of chalk in its mouth. The snake would write answers to questions on the blackboard. When finished, Willard would quickly remove the flowerbox, snake and all. He opened the drawer in front of the table and took out a book, torch, crown, and white robe... placing these items on top of the drum, he would lower the canopy and almost immediately fire his pistol. Whereupon, instead of the canopy rising again, it would open out across the back of the illusion and across the stage revealing a very large American flag with Willard's wife, Joy, standing in the center dressed as the "Statue of Liberty."

Following the death of Joy Willard, Harry gave me the "Goddess and the Reptile." It was in poor condition. The beautifully turned metal legs had deteriorated due to rust and age. Mirrors had to be replaced and lights rewired. My grandfather made new legs for it out of 4 x 4's. We reworked the whole trick. After putting it in very good condition again, I tried including it in several of my programs. It always fell flat. No one could get up out of the sitting position and climb up through the trap on top without the illusion shaking so much that it would "give away" what was happening. Many tried but none could do it as effortlessly as Joy Willard. One girl, Eva Jane Robinson, a ballet dancer, came close but not close enough. I stopped doing the trick. Later, I thought it might be a good idea to put bells, a tambourine, chains, etc. on top of the drum and change the flag to a dungeon backdrop. After some "spirit" did all the ghostly things with the items on top, the curtain would open revealing a female dressed as a vampire in long stringy black hair and fang-like teeth. I rigged it up to do just that but never actually performed it.

To see Willard and Joy perform together was really something to behold. The two of them worked in unison as if by clockwork. It was high precision and seemed as though each could read the others mind. When she died, a large part of Harry died with her. To see them on stage together was something that I was convinced I would never see again. I was wrong because it is like that with my wife Joyce (also Joy for short)...hmm...peculiar. My Joy, from the very

56

first time she did it, did not have to be told anything. She just naturally did it as if by some sixth sense. It is, to this very day, really uncanny to watch her. It is as if she were born to do it. I never told her this. Hell, she is hard enough to live with as it is.

Willard was certainly a man of many wonders. I always wondered how he could capture such vast audiences on personality alone. I wondered at his manual dexterity. I wondered at his perseverance. I wondered how in the hell he even stood up with all that booze... but he did and he did it very, very well. There will really never be another like Harry. As I go to my grave I will hear those immortal words, "Hey bud, come on.... let's go get a beer!"

Chapter 16

HOW I BECAME BRANDON

Charles A. "Kid" Koster was the Dean of American Press Agents. He was also seen doing general agent's work. He had represented a very large number of stars of both the silver screen and Broadway. Koster had handled such as Billy Rose's Aquacade, Barnum and Bailey, Mae West, Tallulah Bankhead, Barbara Stanwyck, Frank Fay, Eddie Bracken, Jeffrey Lynn, Bob Hope's tours for '47, '48, and '49, plus over 100 other Broadway stage attractions.

Koster thought that he needed a really big legitimate theatre style magical extravaganza. He found that Dante was out of the business except for an occasional movie role. He contacted Lon Ramsdell whom he had known for a long time. Ramsdell was the general manager for Blackstone the Magician. Koster wanted Ramsdell to let him share the contracting agents chores with George Alabama Florida (that was his real name) who was doing the booking at that time. Koster really wanted this in order to round out the group of other attractions which he was already booking. Ramsdell turned him down cold. This made Koster mad since he was not used to being told "no." He decided to create a show of his own and he wanted to use Orpheus as a name. He then thought that was too close in relationship to Hell, so he settled on the name Brandon taken after a

Saint. Koster created the title "The Amazing Brandon and His Spectacular Arabian Nights Revue...1001 Wonders of Baghdad." Then he advertised in Variety and Billboard for an illusionist that could fill the bill. A fellow that worked under the title, "The Amazing Milo" and sometimes "Milo and Roger the Men from Mars". As strange as it seems Milo's real name was Arthur Brandon. He never worked under the name Brandon, always Milo. Koster thought it over and decided he had better see the man perform before investing big money in him. I think he booked him in a school in Marysville, California.

The performance proved to be a disaster. Koster had an interest in one of the big show printing establishments and I think they were out on Western Avenue in Los Angeles. He had the artists lay out and make "blocks for 14x22's, 22x28's, one sheets, three sheets, six sheets, and 24 sheet billboards, and they printed a ton of it. It was beautiful multi-colored posters. *(See Appendix A-6)*

Koster asked Floyd Thayer of Thayer Magic Manufacturing what he should do and Thayer told him about Willard. Koster had a partner named Harry Landers. Landers wife was the personal secretary of Anne Baxter who was a well-known screen actress in the '40's and '50's. Both Koster and Landers came to San Antonio. They could not locate Willard but were told, at the magic store, that if anyone could find him it would be me. That is why they called on me. We found Harry showing for the Volunteer Fire Department down in Pleasanton, Texas. Koster offered him a really splendid proposition. Harry simply said , "If it means going outside of the four states in which I am best known, I am not interested." Without my knowing it, Willard took him aside and told him that I was just as capable as he was going to find. Koster convinced me to try it. He booked and billed me all over the Western part of the United States. It went well enough so he wanted me to agree to sign on for a second go round which I refused. I had another bee in my bonnet. It was called "spooks."

Koster said he had no use for the paper without me and that if I could pay the costs of shipping the paper to any address I wished, then I could have it as well as the name and the title. He put that proposition in writing. He felt that I had established the name and no other. People in all of those towns knew me as being "it." I really did proposition in writing. He felt that I had established the name and no other. People in all of those towns knew me as being "it." I really did not think so. I believed that any half capable performer could carry it off because the title sold the show. Nevertheless, that is how I became BRANDON and have been ever since.

Chapter 17

MORE PEOPLE IN AND OUT
OF MY LIFE

There were two girls that tap danced on the camp shows with us. One was named Nancy Langford and the other was "Toots" Johnson. *(See Appendix A-7)* After the close of World War II, Toots opened a dance studio which flourished throughout the '50's and '60's. I do not know what happened to her. Both girls were much better magician's assistants than they were dancers. The men in uniform did not care whether they could dance or not. I think that they were really only interested in seeing as much of the female leg and anatomy, unobscured, as possible.

Nancy Langford took a shine to me. I never could see why but she did. It might have become serious except for the fact that one time, when we had a week off, I took her over and introduced her to my mother. That was the end of that. Boy, I thought World War III had begun.

Nancy Langford had a tap dance outfit that was covered with little bells, which jingled when she tapped. Not in unison--it was just racket. One time I was ready to walk on stage and commence doing magic. I had a dove in my sleeve and tanks of cigarettes for

61

producing out of the air pinned inside my coat. There were flowers and magic gimmicks all over me. Nancy ran up and started kissing me and hugging me. I pushed her off. This was during a very serious part of the show. It was so quiet while the company manager was giving a prayer, Nancy ruined it. I asked her not to do that again. I also suggested that she not wear the bells anymore. It made no difference what I said because the manager told her that if she ever wore that outfit again she was through. It was just as well because the bells did not help anyway. Those cigarette tanks that I wore to do the cigarette trick turned me against smoking.

I had saved and saved until I had enough to buy a set of white tails. This was a beautiful full dress suit that had to be made in England. I always counted the 20 cigarettes in each tank. On this one occasion I miscounted. One cigarette was left burning and sticking out of the holder. I had finished the act, took off the coat, and tossed it on a chair. It was a miserably hot day in the summer, so I think I went for a Coke to try and cool off. When I came back I found the coat with a huge smoldering hole in the front left side leading up to the breast pocket. I tried, but the material could not be matched for purpose of repair. It was a real loss. I was so damn mad I never smoked again.

Willard did not use a tank for the cigarettes. He would just dump some in each pocket and "steal" them, one at a time, while the audiences attention was directed elsewhere. Today, if I have to do the trick, I do it his way. So does John Calvert. John was a great admirer of Willard and hung around him.

Elburn Calvert grew up in Indiana and Ohio but his prominence in performing his magic shows took place in Kentucky, Tennessee, Arkansas, Louisiana, and Texas. He changed his name to John early on because, rightly so, Elburn just did not seem to fit with the title of a magician. John Calvert strongly thought it to be an altogether good idea to be a movie star. So he developed the appearance and demeanor of a motion picture artist. Between appearing in some "B" (second rate) pictures he always went back to performing his magic show. He presented a powerful stage personality. He had a fine voice, he sang, and he was a "handsome devil." John never achieved the pinnacle of success to which he aspired. He was fighting Blackstone's show, Dante's show, and

Willard. Still, I, along with many others, always viewed him as one of the great luminaries of the magic world. He is the only magician that I ever saw that could actually "sleeve" a salt shaker. He could hold the shaker between his thumb and first finger and snap those fingers as the shaker visibly disappeared (up his sleeve). John's biggest break came when he took over the movie role as the "Falcon," a popular detective. Actor Tom Conway had played the "Falcon" up until that time. Conway was the brother of the famous screen actor George Sanders. Actually John found enough "admirers" who were willing to invest the money for him to purchase the copyrighted title to the "Falcon" and the old Nassour Brothers studio. Nassour was famous for its Travelogues. John made several Falcon movies and then left the United States for a world tour in his 112' boat... which later sank. Everyone always waited to see what John was going to pull next. His exploits alone have filled a book.

Calvert had several ghost shows. I seem to recall his having a unit of Kroger Babb's "Chasms of Spasms" show and later "Dr. London's Inner Sactum" ghost show. He always liked to do the "Dr. Q" hypnotic stage act but he added a stunt that many still consider extremely dangerous. He would usually try and find the biggest, toughest looking member of the audience and dare that person to come up on stage. He would tell the man that he was going to put him to sleep. After making some hypnotic passes, and with John's right hand on the man's throat, the subject dropped to the floor and really looked lifeless. Usually the victim was a much larger man than Calvert. What he was doing was applying pressure to the carotid arteries in the man's neck which instantly and temporarily cut off the blood supply to the brain and the subject would, quite literally, "pass out." A little too much of this diminished blood to the brain could have proven disastrous.

I would imagine that John Calvert is now probably somewhere around 85 years old; nevertheless, at last report he was still performing. He had a long run at the Holiday Inn in the Grand Cayman Islands and may, for all I know, still be there. I knew Calvert in this country. I never saw him give a bad magical performance although, as with everyone, some were much better than others.

Bobby Kershaw played the bass fiddle on our camp show unit. He was much smaller than the fiddle. He wore a little green hat over his shocking, crew- cut white hair. He would dance around the fiddle while he played. Audiences were more interested in watching him than listening to him. He taught me to slap a bass. I could play trap drums and sometime, just for grins, he would hold his bass and I would tap out a drum solo on the strings of the bass while he pretended to rest.

Sam "Shorty" Hamilton was with us. He played a piano, when there was a piano to play, otherwise he played an accordion. Shorty was the only human being that could actually play a piano upside down. I do not mean that the piano was upside down--I mean Shorty was upside down because he carried a little, well-padded stool that elevated his head about one foot above the floor. He would stand on his head on that stool and play the piano while he was upside down... and very well, too. In addition the musicians played the background music for the acts but they doubled in brass by doing an act... frequently with their musical instrument. One fellow put on a hand puppet and let the puppet push the valves on his cornet as he played it. The rest of the stage was dark and the little puppet looked cute struggling to push some of them down. His name was Frank but his last name escapes me. I ran across him so many years later at a magic convention in Austin, Texas. I reminded him of it and he was pleased that someone remembered. He had become successful in the jewelry business. I think his last name was Mann.

Danny Dreeson was a hoofer/juggler who was a dear friend and a great act. He introduced me to Eddie Grady. Eddie was drummer with Glen Gray's "Casa Loma" orchestra. They were playing at the Anachaco Room of the St. Anthony Hotel. Eddie and Danny both lived at the Elks Club. Eddie taught me to be a drummer. Every day for a period of one or two hours I went over to his place for instruction. I was a pretty fast learner. I had a set of traps at home and practiced daily until neighbors would, in desperation, call the police... I was a hell of a nuisance. One day I went to Eddie's for my lesson... he came to the door and the whites of his eyes were yellow. He looked yellow all over. He said that he had been diagnosed with an irreversible liver disease and he was returning to his home back east immediately... to die. I never saw nor heard of him again.

Danny was playing a week at the Majestic theatre and wanted

me to see the show. He would juggle indian clubs, balls of all sorts including the tennis variety, rings, square and oblong blocks, etc. He did all of this while he was tap dancing. Near the end of his act the telephone would ring, and while he continued to dance and juggle, he pretended to be talking to the stage manager who was telling him to hurry because they were running late. Whereupon Danny would hang up and juggle and dance twice as fast. In recent years I have seen a young comic on several television talk shows. I think his name is Tom Dreeson and I have always wondered if he is any relation to Danny Dreeson because they look very similar.

During the same week Danny was "on" at the Majestic, there was also a comic magician to whom Dan introduced me. This man was as good as Cardini without the gloves and monocle. He told me that he could not make it doing straight magic, although he was one of the best manipulators I ever saw. Amazingly when he began screwing everything up, his whole life changed... for the better. His name was Carl Ballantine and he later became known internationally as Gruber on the television series, "McHale's Navy." He has enjoyed great success and deserves it.

Chapter 18

BIG TIME GHOSTS ET AL

It must have been somewhere in the mid-forties because I was still doing the camp shows at military installations when several of us went to see the "Durso" show. Not having seen any of the advance publicity and promotion of this show I had absolutely no idea what to expect. All that Harry would say about it was that it was a "spooker." The show was to be held at the Cameo Theatre on East Commerce Street in San Antonio. This theatre was part of a chain of theatres which, I think, was nationwide and all Negro houses. In those days every "white" theatre had a "black" balcony or segregated section for Negro patrons only. Usually there was a separate box office and entrance for blacks. Then there were also theatres for "blacks only." As reprehensible as it was, that happened to be the sad state of affairs as they existed during the dark period in our history. Well the Cameo was a part of this chain that operated theatres in most every state. I had not considered the possibility that we would not be granted admission. We were not. Willard asked the manager to allow him to speak to Mr. Steed. Harry was taken backstage. In short order a miraculous change occurred. We were not only ushered in without paying an admission, but we were given a special row of seats just for us. It turned out that Harry had known Steed after he (Steed) had

66

attended a couple of Willard's performances in Louisiana. Steed used the professional stage name of "Durso." I could be incorrect about his last name--it may have been Steel but I am sure that it was one or the other. The show started and was pretty much standard magic with the exception of a really hilarious hypnotic routine using volunteers and stooges from the audience. Throughout the show the magician made constant reference to, and made threats that, unless the audience remained seated and quiet, that he was going to turn his fiends, ghouls, monsters and ghosts loose on them out in the auditorium. I laughed at the thought but that is exactly what he did.

The finale of the show produced a cremation in the form of a coffin and from that thing came several really hideous looking creatures which started down the steps into the audience whereupon all of the lights, not just on the stage but out in the auditorium proper, went out. That included the restroom lights, foyer, etc. This was a large theatre. Suddenly all over the theatre big hands would appear and would grab at the people from the ceiling, giant spiders would crawl over the seats after them, formless "ghosts" would fly, back and forth, the entire length of the auditorium, and vampire bats would dive on the seatholders. Screams mixed with the horrible sounds coming from the sound system added to the mayhem. When the lights came back on there were people down between the seats, standing, crying, trying to run, and some had actually fainted.

This started me thinking about an elaboration on such a theme. I did not feel that standard magic was congruent with a ghost show; but, I did think that some items could be re-vamped and converted to such a thing. It would be a real tour de force but that was what I did. There was an insidiousness about it but I never got over it. The next day I started writing down which magical illusions might be adapted and it turned out that there were more than I originally thought. More about that later on. I have been told by my dear old friend, David Price, official historian of the International Brotherhood of Magicians, that "Durso" was, in fact, T.V. Steede of Thomasville, North Carolina and that he died in 1955. *(See Appendix A-8)*

I started with an old guillotine which Harry had given me. This illusion was gigantic. It was very heavy even when disassembled and in a sorry state of disrepair. Essentially the trick provided for a person to be placed behind the illusion and their head and hands placed in stocks. The huge blade weighed almost 90 pounds and it had, at great expense, to be re-chromed. When the blade was hauled up to the top of the nine foot frame, by winch and cable, it was locked in position to drop. A basket was laughingly placed on the floor beneath the head. While the magician was talking to the audience and seemingly, not noticing what was happening, an assistant dressed as a hunchback with a terribly distorted face, came out and tripped the release. The blade fell, blood flew everywhere and the head fell into the basket. Spectators actually saw the head fall. The hunchback picked up the head in one hand and a very evil looking knife in the other... headed down into the audience when the blackout occurred and the ghosts came out. This was the feature of my first spook show. That show was titled, "The Mad Doctor and his Chamber of Horrors." As with Steede's show, we did terrific business. Long, long lines were left standing after the theatre was packed full. Since the show went on at midnight it was impractical to ask potential patrons to wait for a second show because they would have been left standing for two hours or more and the second performance would not commence until approximately two o'clock in the morning. We were doing such a fantastic business that the theatre managers started insisting on us playing all week long and midnight performances on Fridays and Saturdays. We had no shows on Sunday. In those days, particularly in the bible belt, "blue" laws prohibited it.

My first Mad Doctor (hunchback) was T. O. "Jack" Burroughs. Jack had been a stunt rider in western film and a rodeo rider in his younger days. I met Burroughs while he was living at the old "Cactus" hotel on South Flores Street in San Antonio. Burroughs introduced me to a friend from his movie days named Lee Morgan. Morgan had over 1,300 films to his credit. He had played everything, werewolves, vampires, all kinds of monsters, cowboy in "B" western films, etc. Morgan looked almost exactly like Lon Chaney, Jr. and had been his stand in. *(See Appendix A-9)*

The second season of the show was featuring Lee Morgan as the Wolfman. Two other changes occurred that year. I seem to recall that it was 1947 and Jack David Goldman (who changed his name to Tiger) was president of Global Productions. *(See Appendix A-10)* Jack Tiger had familial connections to some executives with a couple of the really big motion picture chains. He had booked a number of "live" attractions into large numbers of theatres. Tiger came to see our show in Los Angeles. He came back after the night performance and told me that ours was the first ghost show he had ever seen. He fell in love with it... particularly the box office it was doing. He wanted to represent the show. Because of the reputation which the show was developing the attraction practically sold itself. Nevertheless, we had to have a man go ahead of the show and book and route the dates. A man named J.W. "Jimmie" Richardson was handling the booking chore at the time. Richardson had been an embalmer with a mortuary in Fort Worth, Texas, when he came to work with us. Richardson was very greedy and was being paid 50% of the show. He did not have a contract just an employment agreement sealed with a handshake. I told Tiger we were in no position to avail ourselves of his services unless he wanted to buy Richardson out of his job. Tiger said that if we would help him accomplish this, he would be willing to book and promote the show for 35%. I was astounded to find that Richardson literally jumped at the opportunity. What I did not know was that Richardson had been planning, all along, to frame a ghost show of his own so that he could keep all of the money. Richardson tried it with his "Horror Mansion" which never got off the ground although, in order to obtain some bookings, he showed bookers some of my materials and led them to think that, without specifically saying so, they were actually booking our show. I never saw Richardson's show, but I was told by some of the bookers and buyers that it was so bad that in some cases they paid him off not to perform.

Tiger proved to be a wise choice. We remained together for the next several years. Tiger booked us into over 2,600 top flight "A" houses. It was Tiger, and Tiger alone, that got us into Paramount houses, Fox houses, United Artists houses, and Martin Theatres of Georgia, Alabama, and Florida. With a simple telephone call he could arrange a full year's work. Tiger did all of the booking and business by telephone. It was not necessary for him to go out on the road--an ability from which he profited greatly. We changed the name of the show to "Brandon's Tomb of Terror" which was my sole creation. *(See Appendix A-11)* We changed the entire show and its feature each year--always trying to outdo the previous year. Season's features variously included the Wolfman, Frankenstein's Monster, Dracula, Zombies, and hordes of others.

One season we featured the giant "Gorilla" a mad, vicious monster with the strength of ten men. Let me explain how we used it. This giant chrome cage was rolled on stage, a girl placed inside, a gun fired, and the girl changed into this really big horrible gorilla with fangs. The front of the cage dropped down, the monster ran out and jumped off of the stage into the audience, and all of the lights went out. Someone would scream, "it is loose in the audience." A spotlight on stage would come on for just an instant and they would see him in the balcony. The light would go off and on again only for the ape to be in the middle downstairs. It would happen several times with the gorilla showing up all over the theatre. The audience went wild. What we were really doing was having several men dressed in identical gorilla suits, strategically placed all over the house with pre-aimed spotlights on each one's section. Rotation of illumination created the force and effect. Knocked them out!

A large number of situations would set it up so that all of the downtown houses were sold out well in advance. We would not have been able to move the show from theatre to theatre so we moved the audiences instead. This was bicycling the audiences. We would do a stage show in our fixed location while the other audiences were being entertained with horror movies in the other theatres. When the first stage show was over, that audience was marched out the doors and lined up at the next theatre and waited for them to come out of the movie. The emerging movie audience would be marched over to where we were and we did a show for them and then that audience could go home while we were preparing for the next one. This worked splendidly and without mishap. Off duty police officers were there for protection. It was not uncommon to see many thousands of people marching down a main street at two or three o'clock in the morning.

The whole thing just kept getting better and better. There were only two or three of us in the beginning. After the first season we had dozens of "copycats" but being first we were established. Others were not so fortunate. One competitor who rode the crest with us was the Dr. Silkini Show. Actually there were two of them. They were foster brothers and their real names were Jack and Wyman Baker. For the really big shows there wasn't any threatening competition. The Bakers' business fell off to almost nothing because they would never change their show. Audiences did not want to see the same show and advertising each season.

I remember one year in Oklahoma City there were three ghost shows playing the same night. We were in the big downtown houses and they were out in the suburbs. Interestingly enough all did turn away business. In addition to Lee Morgan other movie actors made personal monster appearances with ghost shows. Bela Lugosi (as "Dracula") even took out his own spooker.

Glenn Strange who played the role of Frankenstein's monster in the last three Universal films toured with us. Strange also played the part of Sam the Bartender on the television series, "Gunsmoke" for 20 years. I am not sure the personal appearances by stars helped. We were already doing maximum capacity business. How could it get to be any better than that?

We thought that it would never end. We became drunk with the power of our own egos. It really was not us. It was the lure of being alone in a totally dark theatre with a girl, or wife, and enjoying the "fright" together while locked in each others arms. The advertising campaigns were powerful and compelling. The opportunity of seeing what one of the film monsters looked like on stage added to it but the draw was just about the same with or without the movie actors--although them being with us did add, somewhat, to the show's prestige.

The year that it all ended our feature was the "Zombietown Funeral" wherein we had what looked like an open grave in a cemetery setting. This thing was portable and could be slid on and off of the stage. The audience would see the upper edge of a coffin lid open and this "thing" sit bolt upright. This zombie had dark sunken eyes, sunken cheeks, black stringy hair down to his eyebrows, fang-like teeth, and he was covered with calcium phosphorus which made him light up in the dark. He literally glowed green. He, and an assembly of his fellow zombies, descended upon the audience when the lights went out and the seance started. During this show the zombie "Impaler" illusion was highly effective but so gory that we took it out of the show and replaced it with a simple sword penetration.

I had scheduled for the upcoming season a feature entitled, "Voodoo Devil Dolls" with a number of effects using these creatures.

We never got to use them. That was when the anamorphic lens was invented and Cinemascope was created. This required that huge, curved motion picture screens, reaching from wall to wall, had to be built out in front of the stages closing them off permanently.

This was something that came into its own because, by and large, the movie houses were fighting desperately for their very lives. Television was taking its toll. A number of the optical gimmicks were created in an attempt to compete with TV. Cinemascope, Vista Vision, Cinerama, Todd-AO, and even 3-D were tried. None worked very well. The whole thing was an exercise in futility. I have always thought that if these houses would have gone all out to compete using live entertainment of enhanced quality vaudeville-type presentations they would have enjoyed a much better chance because no picture, movie, or television can really compete with the real thing right there before the audience's eyes.

As far as I was concerned by the end of 1953, fully 70% of the houses had converted to some sort of large screen affair that precluded any possibility of further stage use. Some stayed on "beating a dead horse" so to speak. They even wound down to the point of trying to present ghost shows in Drive-In theatres on top of the projection booths. These were pretty dismal. Without the proper stage setting they just died. I went home to San Antonio.

Chapter 19

TELEPHONE PROMOTIONS

My mother, Nancy Estes, was working as the office manager of the San Antonio Elks Club (B.P.O.E.) located on Pecan Street, and she introduced me to a man that was staying there in one of the rooms. His name was Sid Presson. Sid was an advance promotor for the "Clyde Beatty Trained Wild Animal Circus." In turn, Sid Presson introduced me to Jack Knight who was the Clyde Beatty advance contracting agent. It was with Mr. Knight that I became introduced to telephone promotions... something that I would live to regret.

During the winter months, Jack Knight lived in Laredo, Texas. He wanted to know how much I would charge to bring a two-hour magic show to an auditorium and give a matinee and night performance. I did not particularly want to go so I said that I would have to have at least $1,000 plus the expense of transporting the equipment back and forth in addition to motel and food expenses for my crew. I figured that this would scare him off and I would not have to go. The only reason I spoke with him in the first place was to please Sid Presson. I thought about it for a few days and decided that, after all, I knew nothing about Mr. Knight. I started to wonder whether, or not, I was going to be paid. So I called him and told him just that, I told him that I hated to do so but wondered if he would be willing to give me an advance on the money. Mr. Knight said, "I will do better than that... I will wire you all of it." Two hours later I had a Western Union money order for $1,000. He called me back, long distance, and asked if I had received the money. He said to ship the equipment and have it sent C.O.D. and he would pay for it. He would have it delivered onto the stage of Martin High School auditorium the evening before the show. There was just one thing he wanted--my word (even if he were not present) that I would perform both of the shows as though there were full houses even if there was not a single person in the audience.

My crew and I arrived in Laredo at the appointed time. We checked in and then went to the auditorium. The janitor had waited, after the school was closed, to let us in and to show us how to work the lights. Everything went as scheduled. There were several hundred children at the matinee performance. The place would seat about 2,000 people and the audience seemed paltry to me. There were less than 200 people at the evening show. After the show, Jack Knight showed up. I felt embarrassed and really bad for him because of such a poor turnout and I told him so. He commented, "think so... let me tell you something, I cleared over $13,000 on your show here today!" I was flabbergasted. How could such a thing be true??? Then it was all explained to me--well, not quite all.

Mr. Knight told me that, as a side line, he ran promotional telephone campaigns. At first I thought that meant that he did work for the telephone companies. He did not. He, reluctantly I might add, said that he would go into a town and find a charitable sponsor such as a police association, volunteer fireman group, Shriner's, Elks, Lions, or whatever and enter into a contract with them to sponsor a fund raising show. Then his personnel would have a large number of telephones installed in offices. They would man the phones and call every number in the telephone book. They would ask the person being called to buy tickets to the show. If that potential customer could not attend the show they would try and talk him, or her, in to "sponsoring some poor children," who otherwise would not be able to see the show, by purchasing tickets for those unfortunate youngsters. They would sell these tickets in very high numbers. I did not find out until it was all over but the sponsoring organization actually received a very small percentage of the money raised. Usually 10% or less.

74

Sometimes the sponsor was paid nothing at all.

I have one pretty bad flaw. I have a strong tendency to believe that people are telling me the truth. Knight convinced me to make a tour for him. I was to be paid a straight salary as was each of my helpers plus expenses. He put a man in charge of the general operation and the overseeing of all of the telephone promotional managers that actually ran the phone crews. Knight hired the managing editor of the Laredo Times newspaper to go out in advance and actually contract the sponsors and buildings for the shows' various appearances. I really thought it strange that they made no request for "show paper"... posters, ad mats, etc. Still I figured they knew what they were doing. Boy, did they ever!

It turned out that the reason they did not run advertisements about the show was that they did not want anybody to come. They would oversell the seating capacity by five, 10, 15 times or even more. If people were reminded about the date of the show they might all come. Promoters could not afford that. The tickets were sold so far in advance, usually months, and most people would throw them in a drawer or something and forget about them unless reminded.

I played all over Texas, New Mexico, Colorado, Wyoming, Utah, Idaho, Montana, Washington, and Oregon for Jack Knight.

The man in charge was Tom Huftle. Crooked as a snake. Somehow Huftle managed to strip the bank accounts in all the towns and run off and leave everyone stranded. He took thousands and thousands of dollars. I called in some "markers" by requesting some hurry up dates in theatres for the illusion show in order to be free from the financial mess in which I found myself.

My next excursion was with the nicest man I ever met. His name was Carl Reid Balmer. *(See Appendix A-12)* Carl had a tremendous amount of experience in show business. That was especially true in areas of the legit theatre. He had been a professional ballet dancer in his youth. Traveling with a ballet company in Canada he found himself virtually penniless when the ballet found itself in financial ruin. Another male ballet dancer, in that same company, roomed with Balmer and found himself in very bad financial straits, was Vladislaw Mikuluk. The two men were trying to figure out what they could do in order to earn a living. They ran through the possibilities and decided that the best opportunity would be if, somehow, they could stage a large magic show. Neither man knew anything about magic and/or how it was suppose to work. First they decided on a name which was "Madame Dubinsky's International Mystery Show." Then, with the promise of large printing orders to come in the future, they talked a printer into making up some handbills, flyers, letterheads, envelopes, etc. on credit. At a local library they gained a very minor superficial working knowledge of the modus operandi of some magic and illusions. They actually talked the Royal Canadian Mounted Police Unit into sponsoring their show. They engaged the largest and finest indoor arena in the area. They convinced the symphony to play for the production. They had placards on every third bus in Montreal. They garnered large amounts of newspaper space mostly in the form of news and events stories. The newspapers went along because of the RCMP sponsorship. They erected a stage in one end of the arena, blocked off the seats behind the stage, and hung some rented curtains and lights. Then they thought it might be altogether fitting and proper to figure out some kind of a show to present. That was when the real problems began.

Balmer and Mikaluk flipped a coin in order to determine which one would be the magician. Balmer won but then in looking closely at each other it was apparent that Mikaluk looked more like the prevailing idea of what a magician resembled. So Mikaluk was it. Next they planned which tricks they should try to do. In actual performance every trick bombed. They needed helpers so they hired males and females from a dance studio. They practiced for several days and nights, but at performance time it just did not seem to matter. A good illustration would be their version of "SHE" the cremation of a person standing in an upright position and covered with a sheet. The sheet is set on fire and after it burns it is obvious that the "burning" person had vanished only to reappear elsewhere. Mikaluk was to be covered and burned. Then a trunk was to be pulled out on the stage, shown to be empty, a gun fired, and amazingly he would reappear in the trunk. The foregoing was to be accomplished with a trap door in the floor of the stage. Balmer was beneath the stage and was to help him down through the trap under cover of the sheet which contained a fine wire form so that observers would think that he was still standing under the sheet. During the show the trunk was pulled out to the point of one of the trap doors. The trunk did not adequately cover the trap. Mikaluk walked around behind the trunk and promptly fell into his own trap... but not all the way. Balmer was underneath this thing trying to push him back up to stage level. This went on for a bit and the audience was treated to the spectacle of Mikaluk rising and lowering, bobbing up and down, behind the trunk and, eventually, falling all of the way through. Then he came crawling out from under the stage, back on stage, out to the footlights where he just stood and bowed. He kept bowing until the audience started to clap. Spectators realized that if they did not applaud he would stand there all night, if necessary, until they did. In fact that was what he did every trick. When he was finished with it he would just stand there and bow. Well, anyway, the audience did hear good symphony music.

Following the Montreal fiasco and after all the expenses were paid, Balmer and Mikaluk each had several thousand dollars left. They came over to the United States but then parted ways. Mikaluk changed his name to "The Mightly Kara-Kum" and Balmer went to New Jersey where he joined the Hamid-Morton Circus as an agent.

I first met Carl Balmer through my dear old friend Carl Guys. Guys had been a feature writer on a Chicago daily newspaper. He was damn good but the only thing that ever interested him was fishing. When he accumulated enough money to do so he quit his job and moved to Del Rio, Texas. Before this move he divorced his wife. He accepted a job as editor of the Del Rio daily paper. The only reason he did this was so he could fish. The Mexicans in the area named him "El Pescador" for the fisherman. Carl Guys and Carl Balmer became great friends.

My show was playing in Del Rio under the auspices of the Police Association. Guys brought Balmer over to the auditorium and introduced him to me. Balmer was booking and promoting the San Antonio Symphony orchestra at the time. The more we talked the more Balmer and I found that we shared values when it came to the successful operation of a roadshow.

Carl understood the fundamentals of telephone promotion but had never operated one. He wanted to try it but not put all of his eggs in one basket. He wanted to book and promote the show using several techniques. Balmer wanted to book some "flat" dates wherein the sponsor, or presenter, of the show simply paid the show a flat fee and then that sponsor would be responsible for handling the ticket sales, publicity, and rental of the auditorium. He also wanted to sell some contracts based on the principle laid down by the father-in-law of McDonald Birch (Birch the Magician) wherein the sponsor guaranteed sales of X number of tickets to the show and if the sponsor failed to sell that many they would still be responsible for paying the show based upon that guaranteed amount; but, if the ticket sales exceeded the amount the overage would be split between the sponsor and the show. Finally Balmer wanted to try the telephone thing. I agreed with most of it--all except the one whereby the sponsor could get hung for a large guarantee if they failed to sell the agreed number of tickets. Balmer said that (as in the case of "Birch") the show was such a powerful presentation the sponsor would be so pleased with the public response that they would not mind the guarantee.

I agreed that we would go together and try it out in a series of towns within a circle around San Antonio. The first spot was Victoria, Texas, and the Police Association was the sponsor. We did fantastic business with turned-away crowds at matinee performances as well as the evening shows. We worked Arkansas Pass, Wharton, Cuero, Corpus Christi, Alice, Robstown, Eagle Pass, Laredo, and finally San Angelo. We were both so pleased with the partnership that we expanded the territory to include the entire state of Texas and eventually the whole country. Carl made so much money that he and his lady love, Bess Huebner, opened the finest ladies' ready-to-wear shop along the Mexican border. It was the Frontier Dress Shop. Carl and Bess would have married but she was already married. Her husband had been so seriously injured in a train wreck that he was powerless to care for himself. Her husband, Herman Huebner was given a settlement, by the railroad amounting to a great deal of money. He had been an engineer for the Southern Pacific. Bess was tied down with looking after Herman but her heart belonged to Carl.

We stayed in Ardmore, Oklahoma, each season because we not only played that city but we had many good friends there. Elmer Wintin sponsored our show during the time that he was Chief of Police and he continued to do so after he became the Sheriff of that County.

One Sunday afternoon we were not working and decided to drive to Tulsa for the opening of the Cinemascope film "Oklahoma"

78

starring Gordon McRae. Enroute to Tulsa, Carl ran off the road and his station wagon turned upside down. I was thrown out of the car as it went over the 15' embankment. The roof of that station wagon came to rest squarely on top of me. The entire weight of the car was on me--naturally, I could not breath, move, or anything else. It would have killed me had it not been for the fact that I came to rest on a sandy bottom of a dried up creek bed. Had there been a rock under me the weight would have pushed it through me. A passing funeral procession saw what happened and all stopped. The men ran down the hill and about 24 of them actually tilted that car up and off of me enough for me to be dragged out. I remained in the hospital for a long time. A large sack of blood hung over my lungs for weeks and weeks. I may be paying a price for that even today with extreme breathing difficulties and pleurisy.

Carl could not wait around for me to heal. All of the shows had to be cancelled and money refunded. While trying to recuperate I was the first satellite TV station in town. I would do it all--turn on the camera, run around in front and do the news, weather, local sports, etc. I would switch back to network and sit around and read until time to go home. I even sold the advertising. It was fun but no money and too hard.

When I finally recovered to resume the show, Balmer returned and succeeded in knocking out the Shrine circus in many Masonic situations. We had these dates booked all the way from Baton Rouge to Tuscon. At that juncture I was hit with a divorce action that tied up the show, home, and property for 18 months. That action was finally concluded with my having the custody of my son, Don Jr., and my ex-wife getting the home cars, etc. I did, thankfully, manage to retain the show properties. It took its toll. All of those shrine dates had to be cancelled. There were only a couple of shows that we considered capable of satisfying such large audiences. Willard was one of them. He was in a state hospital for alcoholism and a recurrence of his lung problems. As unthinkable as it was, he was nevertheless still getting his hands on booze in that facility. One of the doctors stood so in awe of him that the doctor was bringing the liquor in to him. The other show, "Birch" was contractually tied up in such a way that he could not make the tour. Once again we were forced to cancel all of those contracts. In many cities, very large numbers of tickets had been sold by the professional solicitors. They had already been paid their percentage. We had to "buy" our way out as long as the money lasted. When it ran out, lawsuits were filed against us. As years passed, most of the judgements were not renewed and died in time. Carl went home to Del Rio and helped Bess run the Frontier Dress Shop. He was approached by several manufacturers to handle their lines in Texas, which was what he did successfully for many years. I think he had to stop because he lost his hearing.

Chapter 20

SOME SECRETS OF THE SPOOKS

"Black men" were the real secret of the scary ghost seances which took place in total darkness on the Ghost shows. Ours was no exception. When I say "black" men I do not make any kind of reference to colored, racial, or ethnic people. I mean it as an explanation of the way the "spook workers" were dressed. Male employees on our ghost show were dressed in black velveteen. They wore pull-on velveteen pants with elastic waistbands like the "sweat suits" of today. They had long-sleeved tops of the same material and pull-on type shoe covers also made of velveteen. All was topped off with a hood. Even the eye holes in the hood had black gauze sewn over them preventing even a tiny ray or flash of light reflecting on the whites of their eyes which might give their presence away. As time passed they even elaborated on this by wearing padding underneath, similar to that worn by football players. At one point it even evolved into their wearing helmets. This was more for protection from a possible fall and/or being hit by the "spook" of another "black man." Sometime, whether on purpose or by accident, a patron would leave a foot out in the aisle and the "black men" could trip over it. Even if a light came on, all that could be seen would be a large black clump of something. Each "black man" carried a fishing pole also painted with flat black paint or covered with velveteen. Dangling from the end of the poles were the giant ghosts, spiders, vampire bats, etc. All of these items were continuously flying, even zooming, in weird gyrations all over the theatre. They moved so fast that it was virtually impossible to "get a bead on them."

One "black man" wore a leather belt that was a flat black harness with a socket that allowed the largest end of his pole to fit into and rest. Without having the weight as much of an influencing factor he could concentrate on operating his "ghost" which was the largest and longest pole. By standing in the aisle about midway up and holding the pole parallel to the aisle and bringing the spook from the front end of the house toward the back, astoundingly in total darkness, it looked as though a ghost was zipping from one end of the theatre auditorium to the other. All of this was based on the principle that we humans cannot use our visual depth perception in total darkness. In other words a person watching all of this was unable to tell how close the apparition was, or how far away. The dimensions of the ghostly object could not be determined. We also had people planted in the audience with "extension rods" which were similar in nature to an automobile radio antenna except that they could be extended much longer. These "plants" would have an extension rod and ghost, in its collapsed condition, either in a paper sack, under their coat, or even up a sleeve. The rod was brought out and extended to wave over the heads of the audience. We also used ping pong balls painted with luminous paint so they would light up an eerie green or blue in total darkness. When one of these balls was thrown out into the audience it would land on someone and they would usually scream and throw it off of them onto someone else. On stage we could see these things bouncing all over the theatre. There were literally dozens of other effects which we produced... far too many to list here. Suffice to say that pandemonium always broke out.

Once in Abilene, I could see from the stage that one of the newer "black men" was about midway up the aisle just standing there with his spook dangling. I decided that he had become disoriented; so I felt my way down off the stage and up the aisle, took him by the arm, led him up the aisle and out the front of the theatre. I pulled his hood off and we walked around the corner to the rear of the theatre to gain re-admission. While walking along the building, a good-natured drunk (who was actually too "spaced out" to be driving a car) came over on the wrong side of the street, stopped, and screamed, "Hey... what the hell do you guys want to surrender for?!" The white ghost on the end of the pole looked like a flag of capitulation.

We always carried the following tag lines in all of our advertising: "Only seating capacity will be sold... no one will be allowed to stand... buy your tickets now in order to avoid disappointment." That was baloney... not only did we let them stand we also sold out all of the standing room.

I think the one single greatest mistake that I ever made in my life was agreeing to let two other men go out, under my name, and run units of my show. In a way it was necessary because the bookings and the requests for bookings were so great that we actually had several years' work backed up. A competing show, "Dr. Silkini's Asylum of Horrors," at one time had seven units of that show out on the road.

Wyman Baker (one of the Dr. Silkini's) was a very good friend of mine. Our families liked one another and our paths would frequently cross all over the country. We helped each other and did favors for one another. Once in Ponca City, Oklahoma, Wyman was playing and I was over in Enid. We had early shows and Wyman had a midnight performance. We rushed over to see him. Everyone had quit so just his wife and he were left. We pitched in and helped him do his show. I played the monster for him and my wife worked the super X levitation. In California we would drink together and swap stories. After the spookers ended and Wyman did not know how he was going to make a living, I taught him the telephone solicitation business in so far as it applied to promotional show business. We were very good friends and still are.

Since we had so many bookings stacked up, Tiger convinced me that he could do the show and let him take a unit of "Brandon's Tomb of Terror" to the northeast.

Junius G. ("Pat") Patterson was the truck driver, stage manager, assistant, and jack of all trades for McDonald Birch (Birch the Magician) for many years. I knew Patterson because he stayed with the Birch show while it was at our home in San Antonio. The big semi-trick that Birch had allowed for living quarters in the front end, had a separate entrance, bath, eating and cooking necessaries, and a bed. All that was needed was to tie into some electricity and water which I provided. From day one Patterson wanted into the spook business. He convinced Tiger to help talk me into letting each of them take a unit of the show. I should have been shot for doing it.

We were enroute to a new string of dates and had three days in between so we went over to see Tiger do his show. Worst fiasco I ever saw. He tried to do the spooky dancing handkerchief and somehow managed to get himself all tangled up in the "gimmick." To the audience it looked as though he was trying to do some kind of a weird, frantic ballet dance. They had to close the curtain on him. He should have remained in his forte; he was the best booking agent I ever saw. P-E-R-I-O-D.

The idea for the "black men" came from the days of the "black art shows" wherein a cabinet, as in the case of Howard Thurston (Thurston's Wonder Show of the Universe), a contraption of approximately twelve feet long and eight feet wide on rollers with a completely flat black interior--that included the floor. "Black men" moved freely about inside this cabinet. Various objects floated, changed, and vanished. Some of the most startling stage effects occurred inside this cabinet. At least two small lights, on the front of the cabinet, were necessary in order to confuse the eye of the onlooker. It was done on even more elaborate scales wherein the entire stage was draped in flat, black velvet and that included the floor. The confusing lights were often seen as imitation street lamps which were painted snow white. These were attractive and added to the setting but served the most important function of rendering the "black men" totally invisible. All objects to appear, change, vanish, or float (with the exception of the wonder worker) were painted snow white. Those humans, or animals, intended to be seen were also white.

Kenneth McKinney (Jabo the Singing Monster), toured two or three seasons with both "Brandon's Tomb of Terror" ghost show and "Brandon's Arabian Nights Revue" the full evening illusion show. *(See Appendix A-13)* Ken McKinney has, what I consider to be, the finest voice in America. I would rather listen to him sing than to hear Robert Goulet. He should be ranked up there with people like Frank Sinatra. Just simply beautiful. Regrettably, Ken never thought himself to be that good. Even with his great success on the "Don Ho Show" in Los Vegas, Arthur Godfrey and winning the "Gong Show" three times he did not have enough faith in himself. He did not like his own looks (who really does?) and consequently, his ego strength was insufficient. He could never be made to recognize the fact that he looked much better than, oh say, Al Jolson. Jolson was the "World's Greatest Entertainer" and, in his era, the highest paid. Magnifying the money Jolson earned by today's standards, I suggest he would still be way up there and perhaps still the best and highest paid. His basic appearance was so unattractive that he wore black face minstrel makeup. My God, with a voice like Ken McKinney's who the hell cares what a person looks like? Today McKinney is living in Lexington, Kentucky, and is married to the sister of Jim Varney ("Ernest" of commercials for television and movies and "The Beverly Hillbillies"). Ken has now found that his attitude toward himself has changed. He has great self confidence and he has become a really handsome rascal. He fullfilled over 100 engagements during the 1994 season. He is being seriously considered for two movies, he is at Rupp Arena each year with Carl Hurley's "Cavalcade of Comedy" in Lexington and has been labeled "America's singing senior heart throb" by the Retirement Homes Association.

On my show Ken McKinney was terrific. On the ghost show when we did not have one of the famous movie actors playing the monster roles, McKinney did it. He also drove the truck, helped unload, uncrate, set up, hang scenery, as well as act as an assistant. To see him in a green spotlight in that horrible Frankenstein makeup coming toward you, and suddenly stop to start singing "Some Enchanted Evening is quite an experience. That beautiful voice coming out of that awful looking monster is both beautiful and shocking at the same time.

Charles Lowell Burnes also travelled with us in pretty much the same function as Ken McKinney with the exception of playing the monsters. Chuck was not tall like Ken McKinney so he played the "hunchback" and served in various other capacities including assistant and stage manager. Both men did such outstanding jobs that they will always occupy particularly fond places in both my heart and my memory. Whatever Chuck did he did do it very well.

For many years Chuck Burnes was the events producer for the

John Wayne theatre at Knott's Berry Farm and today he is a well-known booker and producer of attractions for colleges and universities on the West Coast. Together with his wife, Bambi, Chuck operates "Periwinkle Productions" a novelty concern. The Burnes' son Chip (aka Chip Lowell) has earned considerable respect as a magician doing an "act" type presentation.

So many great and near great people started on one or the other of my shows. Sometimes a tear comes to my eye when I think back over those days; but then I think of the days with my wife Joyce that have been much better and I have to smile. More about her and her contributions later.

Chapter 21

FRANKENSTEIN AND OTHER MONSTERS

It would be difficult to determine just how many motion pictures Glenn Strange acted in. I am confident that it would surely be in the thousands. Strange was born and raised in the little west Texas town of Clyde, which is about 15 miles from Abilene. I think that he told me that his mother's name was Sarah. He grew up on a ranch so he was thoroughly familiar with the life of a cowboy. Being well suited to work in Western films he could portray the "heavy," the "wrangler", the "Sheriff," or whatever. He managed double pay because he ofttimes did the stunt work, too. He really needed to work in scenes were he was found to be standing because he was six feet, four inches tall and weighed almost three hundred pounds. It was great with someone like James Arness but with the shorter cowboy stars he dwarfed them. Strange had also been a professional wrestler in his youth; therefore, he could "rough house" with the best of them. As time passed and his speaking roles grew better and better, he commanded larger fees.

Glenn Strange starred as "Frankenstein's Monster" in the last three motion pictures, featuring that character, that were produced by

Universal Pictures Incorporated. Those three films were, "House of Frankenstein," "House of Dracula," and "Abbott and Costello Meet Frankenstein." He starred in many other horror films in which he played a monster including the "Mad Monster" where he was the werewolf. His version of the Frankenstein Monster was, by far, the best.

Boris Karloff was Universal's first monster in the original classic film "Frankenstein." Karloff was the Monster again the "Bride of Frankenstein," and "Son of Frankenstein."

Lon Changey, Jr. played Frankenstein's monster in the picture "Ghost of Frankenstein" and Bela Lugosi was that monster in "Frankenstein Meets the Wolfman." It was at this point that Glenn Strange became the monster. He was, by far, the most horrible of all because his deeply lined face did lend itself, very well indeed, to enhancing the grotesque appearance of the monster. Another thing that added to Strange's portrayal was his immense size. In one scene in the movie, "House of Frankenstein" he picked J. Carrol Nash up by his body, and threw him through a window. In that scene Nash looked like a midget compared to the giant Strange.

When Strange put on the Frankenstein Monster padding, boots, headpiece and coat it was really startling to see. He stood well over seven feet tall and the coat was a size sixty-two. He could not walk straight through the average door; he had to bend his head and turn sideways. Strange was seriously injured in the last Frankenstein picture that he made for Universal. In the final monster scene in the picture "Abbott and Costello Meet Frankenstein," Strange (as the Monster) was following Abbott and Costello out onto a pier. The comics were attempting to flee the wrath of this Monster. The escape is planned in a row boat. Unbeknown to Abbott and Costello the row boat is tied up to the dock and can only go so far and no further. The comedians kept trying to row the boat as Strange picked up 50 gallon oil drums and literally threw them at the boat and its passengers. During the filming of the scene the pier was to collapse and have the Monster fall into the water and drown. The main idea was for the camera to stop filming and Strange was suppose to walk back off the pier and he was to have been replaced with a dummy monster made on a metal frame wearing the suit, boots, and rubber head (mask) identical to that of Strange's. That mask was a real work of art. It was made off the face of Glenn Strange and it was possible to actually see the pores in the face. Well, for some unexplained reason, the pier which was also on fire, collapsed prematurely and Strange fell and broke his left leg in several places... something from which he never fully recovered. Months and months of surgeries, pins and bolts, and an unbelievable amount of orthopedic work did leave Glenn mobile but with great physical difficulty. Strange was paid his salary and medical bills and little or nothing else.

On one occasion, during one of his stints with our show, Strange got up off the hospital gurney and started down into the audience. With the green spotlight on him and this hulking fiend looming much larger than life he decided to pick one of the screaming female volunteers, who had come on stage from the audience, up in his arms. While holding the young lady in that position, she urinated all over him. As it was running down his arm onto the stage, he turned to me and said, "Ain't this the damnedest thing that you ever saw???"

At the theatre in Bryan, Texas, the audience was packed with A&M college students. Another audience was waiting in line, two blocks long out in front of the theatre, to gain admittance to the second show. Four of the A&M football players were on the front row and decided they were going to show this monster up as a phony. Just as Strange started into the audience, all four rushed him. Glenn actually picked one of the boys up over his head and threw him into the other three. As they passed the theatre manager, Mrs. Shulman, at the front door they said, "Let us out of here... that damn thing is something else... he is for real."

Strange's role as "Sam the Bartender" in the Longbranch Saloon on the television series "Gunsmoke" lasted for about 20 years. He became a millionaire off of the residuals. I think that through it all his wife Martha continued to operate her beauty salon in Glendale. Strange had a brother, Billy, who gained recognition as a C&W fiddler (violinist).

Chapter 22

THE MAJORITY OF THE REALLY BIG WILLARD EQUIPMENT AND ME

John Daniel owned and operated "Daniel's Den of Magic" in Pasadena, California. A San Antonio man was in Los Angeles and ingratiated himself to John during a period in which John was recuperating from a broken leg. The man in question wanted to buy "Daniel's Den of Magic" or at least that is what he said. Nevertheless, while John was in the hospital the ingrate went into John's shop and literally took everything, the magic equipment, display cases, lighting, even the toilet tissue from the bathroom. John had traced him back to San Antonio so he and his lifelong friend, "Torchy" Towner came to San Antonio. They were driving an old, dark blue, 4-door Packard automobile. They were actually living in the car. I first met John and the Torch at the Fun & Magic Shop. John needed a place to bathe and clean up. We let them park the Packard in the back yard of our apartment house. He stayed about a week. During that time he asked me to introduce him to Willard. I did. He hung around and spent more and more time with Willard. Seeing the great amount of magic and illusions stored at the Willard home he wanted to buy them. Day after day Harry would go and let John drink beer with him. I could see that John was growing somewhat weary because of Willard's evasive actions in reply to the request to purchase. Harry must have sensed this also because one morning (it was barely dawn) I heard this click, click, clicking on my window. I was upstairs in our garage apartment at the time, so I went over to the window and looked down. There stood Harry throwing pebbles against the window to awaken me. I went to the front door and asked him what brought him at such an ungodly hour. He said, "First I want a cup of coffee and then I want to tell you something." I fixed us coffee and while we were drinking it Harry said, "Don, you know how badly John wants to buy the equipment I have left. I doubt that I could ever handle a big show again--especially all that heavy old stuff--but I have decided that John only wants it in order to take it back to California and disassemble it and then make copies of it. Rather than have every Tom, Dick, and Harry doing it, I thought it would be better if I just gave it to you. I really love John... he is a sweet boy but it would be better off in your hands." With that he gave me the key to his barn.

I had to rent trucks in order to move it. It filled all five of our garages and them some. I put some of it in an old barn that aunts of mine had on their homestead. Harry did not want John to go back to California empty handed. The items John was most interested in would have, as it turned out, been the most difficult to copy. I recall they were Frederick Eugene Powell's Coin Ladder (sand operated), a sedan chair, the model of the Girl in the Drum which my grandfather and Harry built, and one of Harry's Broom Suspensions. Actually this was a Lamp Suspension. Instead of the customary platform with a stool and two brooms placed in vertical positions for the girl to hang on, this model was a lamp, shade, and stool. It differed from all others in that the magician did not first remove the stool leaving the girl assistant suspended by her elbows resting on the two brooms standing upright on the small platform. The conclusion of that trick had the magician taking away one of the brooms and then raising the girl's feet to a horizontal position. There she would hang, apparently floating in space, with only one elbow touching a broom. However, not in this version because no one touched the girl. She would step on the stool and put her elbow on the lamp and then, ever so slowly, her feet would rise up until such time as she rested, in horizontal position whereupon she would make a complete three hundred and sixty degree revolution and then float back down to the original standing position on the stool. John took these items and I took all the rest. Harry kept just enough to do a small show; if need be, he could do it alone. I remember he kept a doll house, sub trunk, card star, card sword, bean trick, rice checkers and orange, inexhaustible bottle, passe, sun and moon, etc.

By adding the equipment which I had from the beautiful Dittmar show, equipment built by my grandfather, things that I had picked up all over the country to the Willard magic I think that a person could well understand that there existed in my possession, a tremendous assortment. With even more to come.

John Daniel later took out his wonderful "Shazzam" show which (primarily because of Frank Sinatra) was of short duration. He finally bought out the remnants of Thayer Magic Manufacturing Company with its worldwide reputation for building the highest quality magical equipment.

At times Willard could be very paranoid. He would develop an idea, no matter how irrational it might be, and simply would not let go of it. I never believed for an instant that John Daniel had unethical intentions. John is just not that kind of a person.

As for the ingrate that took everything out of "Daniel's Den of Magic," well, believe it or not, the last I heard, he was a judge in Texas.

Chapter 23

ALONG THE MEXICAN BORDER...

We played for two weeks in the Rio Grand Valley each year during the "hey day" of the spook shows. All the theatres were well equipped and we did the usual turn away business. As a matter of fact the Mexican people seemed to like the "ghosts" more than any others. I know that sounds impossible since the response was so truly phenomenal everywhere the show played. We went from the Paramount in Brownsville all the way to El Paso one year because the order of our dates had to be reverse. While in El Paso we were approached by the Riojas Brothers who were the execs operating the "Oro" (Gold) Chain of theatres in old Mexico. They had the largest chain of houses down there and it literally blanketed the entire country. They were so impressed with the business we were doing that they wanted to cash in on ghost shows. I felt that they were correct because the Mexican people, to this very day, have very strong beliefs in Curanderos (male witches) and Bruhas (female witches), voodoo, witchcraft, and the like. I agonized over such a tour for several days and I discussed it with some friends who lived in Mexico proper. All agreed that the turn-outs would be great but that the economics would not. It was pointed out to me that the ratio of monetary exchange was so disproportionate that it simply would not be economically feasible. If we filled a 2,000-seat theater we would probably wind up with less than $100 (American) even charging a three peso admission price. It was doubtful that such a price could be successfully charged because the people in Mexico were used to paying 50 to 75 centavos for a seat which frequently included a live stage show.

Frank Strickland was the attorney for Paramount Interstate Theatres. He also ran the theatres in Donna, Texas. Frank was great at kidding and practical jokes. One year while playing for him he took a "ghost" up to the projection booth with him. Then, during the seance blackout he left the booth and started waving the spook over the heads of the people sitting in the balcony. He even bopped a couple on the head with it. Since it was made of very thin luminous cloth it could not possibly hurt anyone but when the lights came on people in the balcony were actually trying to climb over the rail and jump to the lower floor for safety. Strickland laughed so hard that he fell out of his own balcony and broke his arm... badly.

Another time he and one of his projectionist were flying to Dallas in his private plane. Frank had been an ace pilot in World War II; however, he had not piloted a plane since the war. He said his nerves had been too badly "shot" to actually do the piloting. His regular pilot was entirely too ill to fly so Frank decided that he was going to do it. Jimmy was sitting in the cockpit beside him. Jimmy, the projectionist, knew nothing about flying an airplane. Just as they were about to touch down on the runway, Frank broke out in a sweat and simply moved the transferable control over in front of Jimmy and said, " Here, you take it." Jimmy fainted.

Another time, just for grins, they put Jimmy into the trunk of Frank's Cadillac. Then Frank poured catsup all over Jimmy's arm which was purposely left hanging out of the lowered trunk lid. Then Strickland slowly drove his car up and down the main downtown streets of McAllen, Texas. Although he knew many people saw it, absolutely nothing happened. Frank was very disappointed--he had hoped to create a minor riot. No one screamed, called the police, or anything. Giving up in disappointment they decided to go back to Donna. Just as he turned back onto the main highway to Donna, Texas, about 20 cars, state police, sheriff deputies, local police, and even an FBI agent had a road block set up and were waiting for them

94

with drawn guns. Needless to say the minions of the law put a total end to that type of nonsense.

When the end came for the ghost shows we went back several times and played the auditoriums in all of the valley towns. The Fort Brown Civic Center at Brownsville was a wonderful facility for an illusion show. Auguste San Martin was the manager of the auditorium. We became fast friends as a result of all of our appearances there. The last year that we played there was a three-day engagement and San Martin wanted us to go over across the border for dinner. We took the whole cast. My stage manager that season was a fellow named Juan (Johnny) Martinez. A super, capable chap, John warned everyone not to drink the water nor eat any of the fresh fruits or vegetables. Everyone on the show, every single one, all 28 of us came down with "Montezuma's Revenge." Johnny and San Martin were the worst of all. San Martin's father owned a pharmacy and sent us over large quantities of Kaopectate and Paregoric. We did a show that night but for the life of me I do not know how. There were 28 of us and only two bathrooms... you figure it out.

Chapter 24

A VANISHING ELEPHANT AND OTHER LARGE ITEMS

Very often, nowadays, people ask me how it is possible for a magician to make a Lear jet vanish? *(See Appendix B-10)* I will answer that for you but I do not want to get too far ahead of myself so let me relate the elephant episode first.

Richard Clemmens (aka Dick Darleeng) was in the business of large animals. Some were wild... so was Dick. He wanted to use the name Darleeng because he wanted to sound East Indian or Hindu. He called us while we were at the Ambassador Hotel in Dallas. We had a two-week layover between tours. Dick said, "I have got the greatest publicity gimmick in the world for you. I can get you a midget elephant. You can do the vanishing elephant stunt. This creature is so cute he will produce all kinds of free publicity." We rented an animal trailer and drove all the way to Florida and back with the little elephant. Incidently, he was not the grey color you normally associate with elephants. This little fellow was black. Dick was correct--he was lovable. He would come up behind you and put his trunk over your shoulder and rub your cheek with the tip of it.

We had a low-boy furniture type van and a K-11 International cab truck. The semi-trailer had two doors at the rear and a big double door in the side. We had a stall built right in the center for the elephant so he could be led directly up a very low ramp into the stall and could easily be backed out the same way. Around this stall were permanent shelves with lips on the edges to keep the cages for the other livestock from sliding off. We had canaries, doves, ducks, rabbits, rats, etc. We were almost a small traveling zoo. When we arrived in a town we would find a small boy (preferably brown or black), wrap a Turkish towel around his head, put a loin cloth on him, and have him, with the elephant, at a parking meter near the auditorium or theatre where we were appearing. Then we would frame it up with a local newspaperman and police officer to meet at the site and the policeman was to issue a summons to the child for "illegally parking an elephant." This worked very well. In just about every spot we would garner great news coverage and often made the front page.

Don't you ever believe that there is such a thing as a midget elephant! By the time the second season rolled around we simply could not get that elephant into the truck. I had to leave him behind near Jourdanton, Texas, with friends, and pay to have him fed, watered, and cleaned up after for seven months. I tried all over to sell him--no one wanted to take him. Finally Balmer got rid of him through a private organization in northern California... maybe Tarzana.

Anyway the method of vanishing the elephant employed by us was very convincing, and most likely, the one used to vanish an airplane. Let me explain. On stage there were back set pieces representative of a jungle setting. There were several trees forefront. Behind two of the trees were vertical piano hinges that ran the full length of the flat. This section opened in the middle and it swung wide to allow the elephant to be taken out through these doors in the scenery and they closed behind the elephant. The doors were very carefully disguised so that the audience could not tell they existed. Directly in front of the place that opened in the scenery was a small platform which stood about 14" high and was in the center of the stage. Unknown to the audience was another platform, in reality a shell, that covered the first platform. The shell had very, very small ball bearing wheels on its four legs. There was a cable attached to this outer shell platform so that it could be pulled, sideways, through the section that opened up in the background scenery. The little elephant would be on the outer platform. He wore a very attractive green and gold harness and the straps coming off the harness were attached to the platform all the way around. A large screen (really just a huge sheet) was lowered from the fly gallery between the elephant and the audience. When the front curtain was opened there stood the little elephant on his platform. The screen was lowered in front of him. A spotlight was turned on that showed the silhouette of the elephant on the screen (sheet). In the meantime the elephant had been pulled out through the back and the doors closed back and no one could ever tell what had happened because what looked like the original platform was still there, laying on it was a duplicate harness and straps but no elephant. Then all that had to be done was to fire the gun, have the spotlight go out, and the screen go up and the elephant would be gone.

Now, visualize if you will a jet plane sitting in front of a background of, oh, let's say scaffolds wherein the audience thinks that everyone is seeing through these scaffolds to an airplane hangar on the other side. What they are seeing is a fake duplicate of what is behind the scaffolds. These scaffolds would open up just as our jungle set pieces did. They would swing open and allow the plane to be pulled off sideways, then the secret doors would close. A huge screen was lowered in front of the plane and a spotlight turned on with the tiny, miniature cut out of the plane in front of the spotlight and the spot projects the image, enlarged to the size of the real plane because of the spot's distance from the screen, and everyone sees projected on that screen the full-sized airplane's silhouette. A group of about 50 volunteers comes up from the audience to stand in a circle around the airplane before it vanishes. The thing is that only half of the volunteers are for real. The other 25 are really stooges working for the magician... once the screen is lowered they let go of each others hands and crowd up together and the plane is pulled out between them. Then these fake volunteers regain their former positions and hold hands again and complete the circle around the plane. The screen goes up, the spotlight goes off, and the plane is gone with the volunteers swearing that they did not see it go.

Chapter 25

THE NEW BREED

With the closing of large numbers of the nation's major theatres, television gained its strongest hold on the attention of the American public. The Sherman Anti-Trust action which ultimately resulted in a "divorce" decision ordered by the Supreme Court of the United States, really meant that the gigantic theatre chains owned and/or controlled by the major motion picture studios, were forced to divest themselves of their theatres or any interest in any monopoly situations. In virtually every market these circuits of theatres owned so many of the houses that they could literally freeze out competition or reduce it to second and third runs of a picture long after the studio chains had reaped the huge profits from the initial exposure.

In San Antonio, Texas, as an example, the Interstate Division of Paramount Theatres operated 28 houses. The few independent houses could only lay claim to a marginal existence.

The "vanishing act" of these wonderful old theatres and their great stages made anything ever done by any magician pale by comparison. Up until this time most families spent a part of their income on entertainment. That entertainment was usually the movies. Off to see the latest that Hollywood had to offer was a weekly American ritual.

Suddenly Americans were no longer asked to pay for that type of entertainment. With the television in every living room the public saw pretty good fare, all for free. The family could apply the entertainment budget to other things. G-R-E-A-T!

The quality was not there, however. The splendor, scope, and production techniques of Hollywood were vanishing. I do not think they will ever return.

Something else happened. The rapport that frequently occurred when these theatres presented live stage shows vanished. The shows just simply were not around to teach, among other things, theatrical obedience; by that I mean when to laugh, when to cry, when to applaud, and most of all, when to be quiet. In today's world the only basic exposure of any importance is at athletic games where everyone yells, screams, runs around and acts really wild. They carry this over to the rock concerts. The shows with "smaltz" that really reached out and grabbed you are gone. The kind of a show that made such an impact upon you that you would really remember it, vividly, for the rest of your life simply disappeared.

The magic scene was dramatically altered, too. The Dante show was gone. The Blackstone show could only play in such a limited number of spots that any profit was impossible and Harry's health would not have sustained a lengthy tour. Calvert left the United States due to tax and other legal problems. Birch retired. Willard's tuberculosis and alcoholism literally crippled him. Virgil never caught on with the audiences. The great ghost show magicians were without their stages and multiple theatres for cross-plugging to draw the fantastic crowds.

The major magic manufacturers never had the market to generate the millions for which they all longed. Most young people saw great magicians as "older" people, usually with white hair, powerfully charismatic, compelling voices, unique deportment, and bearing whose tenor inspired awe. These young people were fearful of aspiring to such a stature simply because of the temporal investment it would require and the "I want it all... now" mentality. The creators and builders of magic and illusions seized upon this opportunity to convince practically everyone that all they needed was a "zig-zag lady" in their bedrooms and some bizarre clothing covered with rhinestones to become an overnight sensation. If these stellar performers would add screaming loud rock racket (I refuse to dignify it by calling it music) and some bright, trailing, flashing lights the success of their careers would be doubly secure. I would point out that if you take a child at the age of two and lock him in a closet and then speak nothing but Chinese to him all of his life he will obviously come out of that closet speaking Chinese. In other words, most have been brain-washed into believing this is MAGIC.

Just try selling that in some of the cities that have had an exposure to both kinds of "entertainment." By both I mean the "new" and the "old." There is absolutely no comparison. They literally walk out on the "Magic of Rock 'n Roll" as in Davenport, Iowa. They know the difference. They "boo" such things. If the new breed of magic were all it is cracked up to be the "Magic Land of Alakazam" would still be on television.

Chapter 26

LOUIS BERKIE, THE FUN & MAGIC SHOP, AND THE ELBEE COMPANY

During the latter '30's, Harry Willard did just fine. As he crossed over into the 40's he started down the slippery slope of fate and a series of disasters.

The first fire destroying the magnificent Willard show was in Kennedy, Texas. The second fire was in La Grange, Texas in 1946. The perilous times that followed reeked of tragedy. If Harry would have allowed his son, Howard, to handle the business and Harry do the performing there is not the slightest question of great success. That wasn't the case. Harry treated Howard as peculiarly as he did me. The disenchantment that arose was very difficult on all concerned.

During the early 40's Harry also abandoned his love of the Mulberry Inn. My grandfather had closed his shop and moved. Harry did little driving in the city. Mostly, he relied on others to take him where he wanted to go or he rode the bus. He acquainted himself with places to imbibe along the bus route from Truax Street to downtown San Antonio. It was during this time that Harry first met our beloved mutual friend Louis Berkie. *(See Appendix A-14)*

Louis Berkowitz changed his name to Berkie when he got out of the service. Berkie and his mother had operated a small neighborhood variety store on South Flores Street near the Willard home. Although Willard had been in his store when he needed an item of the five and dime variety, the two men had never formally met.

Later in the '40's, Berkie moved out on Zarzamora Street which was a long way from his pervious location on South Flores. As with me, there were periods of time that were quite lengthy wherein we did not see Willard. It was during just such a period that Berkie moved again. This time it was to Blanco Road across from a public school. I had a long tour that year. Now Berkie was primarily operating a soda fountain and hamburger joint. He advertised 10-cent hamburgers. He managed to do this by taking a pound of hamburger meat and using fillings and rolling it into small balls which he would place between two sheets of wax paper. Then he would take a rolling pin and roll the meat balls out into such thin patties that you could almost read a newspaper through them. He would pop them on the grill just long enough to warm the meat all the way through. If he had left them longer, the patty would have shriveled up entirely too small. As soon as the meat was warmed he put it on a bun and added mustard or catsup--no mayonnaise because it spoiled too quickly. These hamburgers were so bad that the school actually put him off limits for lunch periods. However, before and after school was a different matter. Mostly the kids came in to look at the second-hand comic books that were sold for the amazing price of two for a nickel.

Driving by one day, I elected to stop and see what all the commotion was about. It was pretty much odds and ends of cheap variety store material, shaving materials, combs, etc. Over in the corner I spied an interesting looking cardboard box filled with an assortment of small magic tricks, silk scarves, ropes, etc. I struck a conversation with the owner, Mr. Berkie, and he told me that someone had given it to him and simply left it there. He did not seem to know what it was nor what to do with it.

The store was full of kids who had come in after school. I picked up some of the tricks and started doing them for the children. They went crazy over the billiard balls, color changing silk, wand penetration, and the rest. They wanted to know where they could buy these tricks to learn how to do them. That very afternoon I sold the entire boxful for Berkie. He was astonished. He wanted to know how and where he could buy more of the same materials and if I would show him how to do them. I made him a list of tricks that I thought he should order and could learn to do. I gave him the names and addresses of some of the magical manufacturing companies which I knew sold wholesale. Then I left.

A couple of weeks later I was back in town and went by to see Berkie. He had ordered all the things that I suggested and then some. I commenced teaching him how to do things like the ball in vase, cups and balls, magician's nightmare, Svengali deck of cards, etc. He was a fast learner and so I left again.

We were gone on tour for an inordinately long period of time that year. When we finally returned to San Antonio I went to see Berkie, but he was gone. He had moved downtown across from the Greyhound bus station. He now called his store the "Fun and Magic Shop." He had not only sold all of the magic which he had ordered but much, much more. He was keeping the shop open 24 hours each day. At that time there were more service men on the streets of San Antonio at two o'clock in the morning than there were at two o'clock in the afternoon because in and around San Antonio there were 13 major military installations. The young servicemen would buy anything. It was not at all uncommon to sell a gross of Svengali decks in a single day.

During the periods between tours I would go down to help Berkie out. I would demonstrate magic and sell it for him. It was simply too much for the two of us. We took in another demonstrator, then another. Finally there were five demonstrators and Berkie started printing wooden nickels. This is an advertising gimmick extraordinaire. If a small hole is drilled through the wood, a key chain can be put through it. Whenever someone has one of these novelty items and they take out their keys to unlock a door or turn on an ignition, they are forced to look at the advertising. Not like other ads which are generally thrown away.

The nickels and the magic both paid off in a big way. Today Berkie is the "Wooden Nickel King." They have clubs all over. He sells them by the millions to places like McDonald's, the U.S. Air Force, Colonial Williamsburg, major brewing companies, and so on. Berkie has been covered in People Magazine and on national TV. He is the most beloved character I ever met. He is big hearted to a fault. He never met a stranger. His friends and admirers are legion. He was probably the strongest single supporter of Harry Willard. In the process of helping Berkie get his operation going in a really big way, I formed a junior magician's club which met at the "Fun and Magic Shop." Paul Copp, Spencer Lemenager, Claude Crowe, and the others became really fine magicians; but, I do not think any of them followed it as a career. I went around to the schools and gave short demonstrations of magic explaining how well magic worked to bring shy children out of their shells. Berkie developed a clientele of teenagers that was really startling. I remember one local dentist's son who bought over $2,000 worth of magic and who came in years later and sold it back to Berkie for $100.

Years ago Berkie changed the name from "Fun & Magic Shop" to the Elbee Company which thrives today and enjoys a world-wide business and reputation.

After my folks moved from the southside of San Antonio to the northside my grandfather did not see Willard very often. Then when my grandfather died Harry lost one, perhaps the only, true elbow-bending buddy. So Harry developed a close relationship with Berkie. Berkie could not drink alcohol but they were comrades in many other ways. Berkie and Willard were just about the same size. The two of them stood just a little over five feet tall. Berkie could not wear Harry's clothing because Harry had very broad shoulders and Berkie did not.

Even when Harry had fallen on bad times and his health was such that he did not look like he would see another day, Berkie would always find some minor thing that Harry could do, such as pack a box, make a shelf, paint some wooden nickels, etc... anything to have an excuse to pay Harry some money. Even if Harry did not need it, Berkie always made this a top priority.

The 1994 Texas Magic Convention was dedicated to Louis Berkie and his contributions to magic and magicians, which was something long overdue and more than well deserved.

Berkie never married although he dearly loved women. He felt an obligation to stay with and care for his mother. She had no one else. Although she had put him and his sister in a children's home in New Orleans when he was tiny, I think he probably spent most of his life trying to prove to her that the two of them should have remained together... regardless.

Berkie's mother had a really unnatural amount of luck. We could go to a festival at the Herman Sons each year and she would always win at least one ham--sometimes more. That was really crazy because she ran a strictly Kosher household which meant NO PORK. That never seemed to bother Berkie. His mom took to the habit of attending "Bunco Night" each Wednesday at the State Theatre during which winners took home large bags of groceries that had been donated by local grocery merchants. Berkie's mother would simply go up on the stage, whether she had won or not, and stand there until they gave her a bag... usually out of desperation.

I remember Berkie telling us that he never had a pair of comfortable shoes until he became a supply sergeant in the Army. His feet were entirely too disproportionate in size. In the service he could take one shoe of one size and another shoe a size larger and he was in heaven. The world will long remember Louis Berkie!

Berkie will be remembered for his philanthropies but also for what everyone considers to be his scatterbrained activities. Everyone with whom I have ever discussed it says that Berkie has been a great success, "not because of Berkie but in spite of him." His system of bookkeeping is throwing everything into drawers, boxes, haphazard files, and frequently losing the material completely. I remember one time after he had exhausted all of his friends advice, he decided that he needed an "efficiency expert" to straighten out his business. He found just such an "expert" who was highly qualified. The man worked night and day trying to make "heads or tails" of the mess. As quickly as he started to think he was "getting a handle" on it and went home for the day, Berkie would come along, right behind him, and put it all back into such a state of disarray that it became obvious it could never be done. The "expert" had to quit because he actually had a nervous breakdown.

Berkie loved machines. He couldn't operate them but he loved them. He had a whole room full of photocopy machines and another room full of computers. He had "keyed in" a great deal of customer information on a computer program. The idea was rapid retrieval for the purpose of soliciting new orders from old customers. When enough time had expired since a customer had last ordered, the program would alert Berkie and he would then write a letter reminding them that it was time to reorder, how many they ordered

the last time, the amount, whether or not the price had risen, etc...
Berkie, and others, worked for months feeding all of this information
into the machine.   When the end was in sight, one night he
"accidently" erased the entire program.

Some say Berkie does not want solutions. My wife says
Berkie really wants the problems so he has something to talk about to
his friends. That may be true. I remember when he had been putting
down what he thought was right to pay the government on his taxes.
He would always add a little more than he thought he should be
required to pay. Well something did not add up so the IRS decided
to audit him. An agent came to his business and asked if he had all of
his records for the previous five years. Berkie said, "Oh, yes, please
come with me." Berkie took the man to a store room as big as a
freight car.   The room was piled all the way to the ceiling with
cardboard boxes. Berkie proudly announced, "There you are." A
desk was moved in and the agent brought in his calculator and
materials with which to work. There were huge piles of cancelled
checks all mixed together and on various banks. Vast amounts were
unrewarding in the information which they furnished. Each one would
have to be taken to Berkie in order to try and determine what the
check was for, to whom it was written, was it a legitimate business
expense, salary, loan, or what. Most often Berkie would actually
remember. There were tens of thousands of these things. After about
one week the agent became frustrated, to say the least, and he called
in additional assistance from other agents. I think there were four IRS
people, altogether, working on the matter. All four became just as
confused. I think they decided that Berkie really was not trying to
defraud the government; but, even if he was, all of the resources of the
government still probably would not find it. So the agent, somewhat
bewildered, said, "Mr. Berkie you are doing a fine job... just keep up
the good work." Berkie showed him a magic trick and he, with the
others, left never to return.

I think that one of the saddest things I ever heard in my entire
life was when Berkie told me about how and when he and his little
sister, Libbie, had been left in the children's home and were not
allowed to see each other. Actually there were two children's homes
side by side with a fence separating the boys from the girls. They
would tell each other that if someone adopted one but not the other,

someday, somehow, they would find each other. They did. Remarkably each became very successful. Louis in his magic and novelty manufacturing business and Libbie as a well-known psychologist for the United States Army.

Chapter 27

READERS OF MINDS

I never knew his real first name. Everyone simply called him "Bootsy" or "Boots." His last name was Shapiro. Boots was the oldest kid in our neighborhood... at least a year or two older than the rest of us. Since there were no others his age to hang around with, he tolerated us younger ones, and naturally being the oldest, he was the wisest. Whenever we had a problem, Boots was the very first one that we called on. He showed me how to install a new bike chain, shoot my air rifle, make a sling shot, etc. Bootsy had the only china berry tree in the neighborhood. All the guys went over and picked china berries off the tree to shoot in the sling shots. One day while I was over in the Shapiro's backyard, I overheard Bootsy telling another fellow that he "should never think anything in front of a woman or a girl that he did not want them to know"... he even said that, believe it or not, females could actually read males' minds. It is some kind of a secret sixth sense. Females will never admit it???

Boy, that really bothered me. Wow... what if that were true. It would be a wonder if any females in my life would speak to me. The weather had turned chilly. I went home and spread my books out on the living room table to give the appearance of my doing homework. What I was really doing was putting the latest issue of my favorite comic book inside my literature book. The lit book was large.

I could sit there and read my comic and if I heard my grandmother coming, I would turn a few pages and they would hide the comic. I was just sitting down when grandmother said, "I know what you are thinking??? Don't get started on any of your stuff. I want you to go out and take the garbage can off the back porch and put it around in front by the sidewalk so the trash collectors will pick it up tomorrow"... that did it... she admitted it... she knew what I was thinking.

The very next day I was delighted to learn that we were having my favorite food--chicken and dumplings. Grandma always made a great big pot full. We went in to dinner. Then I saw IT. There it was... one of her fabulous pecan cakes. We had big pecan trees that always provided the neighbors as well as ourselves with all the pecans we could use each year. Grandma would grind up the pecans and pour large amounts in the cake batter but then she would add pecans to the thick icing on the cake. Super! So I took only half of a carrot, one small spoonful of green beans, one tiny piece of chicken, and one small dumpling. Grandma looked at me and said, "I know what you are thinking... but you are NOT going to have any cake at all unless you eat a very large plateful of everything else first"... She started piling the "everything" high on my plate. For the very first time in my life I had to really struggle to eat all my chicken and dumplings. When I finished I was amazed to find that I did not care for any of that great cake. It was all because of what she said, SHE KNEW WHAT I WAS THINKING. There it was again. Now I was getting scared. I asked my grandfather, "Pappy," "Is it true that women can read men's minds but will never really admit it?" My granddad started laughing and said, "Where did you hear such nonsense?" I told him that Boots told us but that, in a way, Grandma had verified it. He just kept laughing... I saw that he either did not know the truth or would not tell me. I did not know what to do.

Most mornings I walked to school with Mary Jane Ridgeway. Some days I even carried a couple of her books. On the days I book carried, I walked beside her. Other days I really preferred to walk behind her. I liked the way she moved. It was different from boys. Mostly I wondered what she looked like under her skirt. I had never seen a female naked--I imagined all sorts of things. Now I had to face the fact that either Mary Jane knew what I was thinking and did not care (maybe even liked it) or she just had not picked up on my thoughts in that area as yet. Gosh, what a predicament. I had to know for sure... positive. I got on my bike and went to ask Harry. Harry would know. He knew most everything. I found him in his house car sitting at the table drinking, of all things, a cup of coffee. I asked him, "Harry, I just have to know the truth about this or I will die!"

"That is insane," Harry said... "No one can really read minds... some entertainers such as Harry and Frances Usher or Joe Dunninger claim they can do REAL mind reading but it is all a trick"... Harry asked me to sit down while he explained billit reading, crystal balls, one ahead, palmistry, phrenology, and all the demonstrations of the day that were popular but really designed to either entertain or fleece people. I felt better and started to leave but on the small table by the door there was a stack of correspondence. The most prominent letter, which was on top, had a letterhead that reached out and grabbed me: "MERCEDES CAN READ ANYONE'S MIND... KNOWS YOUR VERY SECRET MOST INNERMOST THOUGHTS"... oh my, there it was, right before my eyes, in bold print... A GENUINE ADMISSION OF TRUTH!

As time passed, my uneasiness over this matter abated but the basic premise lingered for years. Finally, I quit thinking about it... except... once in a while... I still wonder... what if???

Now I wonder about the possibility of women having an even greater secret. Perhaps one that even they do not know is theirs. Perhaps about sex. Only a very few know. Maybe only some teachers of anatomy who do not even recognize it themselves. One that a woman will not even discuss with her mother, sister, best friend less they might be considered a freak or different when the real truth is that it is true of them all but if it ever came to light vast numbers of men would lose interest in them... think about that for a minute. I will not mention it now because it could be the basis of another book... but just think about it.

Chapter 28

REAL JOY IN MY LIFE

A lovely lady walked into my office in response to an advertisement which I had been running in a local newspaper. She had been active in theatre, taught at the university level and had a fantastic group of talents. The second greatest thing about her was that she had an open mind. The number one greatest thing was her eyes. Clear across the room, which was large, I could see the huge eyes. They were surrounded by a terrific orange outfit. She looked G R E A T. Something of a smart ass but that goes with the territory. I decided right then and there that I wanted to marry her. But I did not tell her. I really made her work on that one.

The name of that lady was Joyce Arline Creps. She was from Richmond, Virginia, originally. I cannot really hold that against her. She, I believe, was born to perform magic and puppetry. She denies it of course. I took her to her first performance in Encinal, Texas, without really telling her anything about it. I think such discussion prior to actually doing it serves no useful purpose. As a matter of fact most people become a bundle of nerves just thinking about it. Not Joyce. I would have thought that she had been doing it all of her life. She worked the gimmick on the duck tub perfectly. She does things like the "pyramid production" (one of the most startling tricks in magic) and has never been caught, even by professionals such as John

112

Novak, who were actually looking for the secret "modus Operandi."

During the years that she taught on the faculty of Virginia Commonwealth University, she also served as designer for Barksdale, the oldest and first dinner theatre. It is located at Patrick Henry's hangout tavern near his birthplace in Hanover, County, Virginia. Her outstanding work on such shows as a "Lion in Winter," "Annie Get Your Gun," and so many others is widely remembered. Her work is well documented in the book about Barksdale entitled, "Going On... Barksdale Theatre the First Thirty-One Years."

Joyce knows how a show must look not just from the audience point of view but also that of the professional. Her contributions are limitless. As far as the costume and scenic design I know of no one better, and her knowledge of magic and illusions is also second to none. I dare say that she has created more new and innovative magic than Harry Willard. She, and she alone, elevated me, and my staging a thousandfold, Joyce is the very best when it comes to performing, creating, designing, and actually building magic, illusions, and puppets. She has a complete workshop with many lathes, drill presses, routers, radial arm saws, four different band saws, table saws, scroll saws, grinders, sanders, and a planer that can create wooden beams 12" wide, 12" thick, and 16' long. The thousands of trees, most of which are over 150' tall, have produced a supply of lumber sufficient to build houses and accoutrements.

All of the truly marvelous things about this wife of mine are absolutely true; but, it is likewise correct that she is a terrible cook. We really do always know when dinner is ready because we hear the smoke alarm go off. Pygmies come from the Amazon to dip their poison arrows in Joyce's soup. All of us are entitled to at least one failing. HAH!!

To try and list all of Joyce's talents would be futile. I will leave it by saying that her expertise as an artist and layout artist is just plain superb. She alone is responsible for all of our posters, ticket layouts, letterheads, etc. I am including some samples of her work. During the time that she worked for the newspaper, she worked the layouts for some of the most prestigious businesses in this area, as well as in Wilmington.

Chapter 29

JOE WALSH

Joe Walsh answered a distress advertisement which I ran in the trade papers for a telephone promotor, with his own crew, that could conduct the advance telephone sale of tickets and ads in the program for one of the west Texas cities. The man that had been assigned to handle the town was named Allen Tobel, and he was, without a doubt, the number one producer in that business. He once went into Austin, Texas, for Floyd King and the Clyde Beatty Circus and doubled the gross of the previous year. When the time came for Floyd to settle up with Tobel and pay Allen his bonus percentage, it amounted to several thousands of dollars. After Floyd paid him, Tobel took Floyd up to his hotel room for a drink and during the conversation Tobel lifted up the mattress on the bed and showed King stacks and stacks of collected sales envelopes and he said, "Floyd I sure am glad that you're so happy over the amount of money I generated for you this year because those paid envelopes represent the cash that I stole"... he laughed and walked out. No one would bother to try and prosecute him because, even considering the money he would steal, he made the shows that he worked for entirely too much money. He was the only person that I ever heard of that put the price of his shoe shines on the bill at the hotel in which he was staying and then would turn around and run off without paying the hotel bill.

Anyway let me get back to Joe Walsh. The agent that booked the town was a young man named Monroe Spears. Monroe's father was the United States District Judge for the Western District of Texas. Monroe met Joe Walsh and took him down and rented office space, installed the telephones for the purposes of sales, ordered the printing (tickets, envelopes, receipts, etc.), rented the auditorium, and the like.

Luckily, I had three days off between performances and I was in northern New Mexico. I received a call from the president of the police officer's association in the town in which Joe Walsh was situated. The president said, "Don, if at all possible you had best find a way to rush down here because one of our detectives found a flyer with Joe Walsh's picture on it and it says that he is one of the ten most wanted fugitives." I took the first plane to Dallas and then back to the town in question. When I arrived, there was one hell of a furor because the detective, a very red-headed young officer, insisted in turning Walsh over to the FBI. Someone introduced me to the Chief who was a recently elected official. I asked to speak to Walsh to see if the allegations were true. He said they were. Walsh went on to tell me that his name was not really Walsh, but Joseph Francis O'Day. He said that his parents enjoyed an enviable reputation in the world of circus show business. They were famous trapeze artists and they were the ones about whom the motion picture "Trapeze" had been made starring Gina Lollbridgia, Burt Lancaster, and Tony Curtis. He told me a great deal of his long history, a part of which I will relate to you shortly.

I went back to the Chief of Police and I said, "Chief you're not appointed... your position is that of an elected official. This thing is going to hit the media and they will have a field day with it. Can't you just see it when you come up for re-election... why, they will be saying that here you had one of the most wanted criminal fugitives in America working right in the police department." I went on to say that, in my opinion, the very best thing for everyone concerned was to somehow manage to get Joe Walsh out of town. The young detective started screaming, "Absolutely not... I am going to see to it that he goes to jail and they throw the key away." The chief asked me to please step outside for a moment that he wanted to speak to the officer privately. I did and he did. There was yelling and screaming coming out of that office like you never heard before. Finally the chief came out and said, "Don, take him and do not even let him go to the motel to pick up his belongings... just get him the hell out of town." I rented a car and drove Joe to Big Springs, Texas, which was about 100 miles away. I gave Walsh money and told him to take the bus to Carlsbad, New Mexico, check into the La Caverna Hotel, and wait until I sent him his suitcases. I drove back and took his belongings to the Greyhound Bus station and sent them to him in Carlsbad. When I played Carlsbad, I found that he never picked up his things, I never saw nor heard of him again.

Apparently Walsh had dabbled in virtually every kind of larceny. His outstanding chicanery however was in the area of gambling with cards and dice. What Walsh had managed to do, along with his cohorts was this. He had a Buick automobile in which the floor of the back seat had been altered to accommodate trays of dice. They also had a machine that could engrave the dice used in casinos. Walsh's dice were rigged with something like radar. He had an ex-physics professor with him. They could not do it on every number-- only the larger ones. These dice could electronically produce any high number called for. They would go into a casino and be given a pair of the "give away dice," which such establishments are known for. They constantly gave away used decks of cards and dice. They (Walsh & Company) would then take the monogrammed dice down to the car and make an exact duplicate of the legitimate dice from the gambling house, but with their dice they could control the game. It all came from a belt that one of them wore with a lot of large, old style, hearing aid batteries in it. If the first pass of the dice produced a small number they simply let it go. When a larger number that they could make came up they bet the bundle on it. They never played the same spot two days in a row, but would circulate and make all of them. They would make a second round and then leave town for greener pastures. After a while, places like Las Vegas instituted a policy of checking out consistent big winners. That was true even if each win was in a different location. They would then circulate photos of the miscreants who quickly found themselves in jail or out of town.

After having burned himself out in every such spot in this County, Walsh took his operation to San Juan, Puerto Rico. They only lasted three days. The really big "Jefe" called them in and said,

116

"We do not know exactly what it is that you are doing but we do know it is something. I want you out of here on the next boat or plane... whichever comes first." The Walsh gang left and had to leave their Buick behind. Although it was promised that the car would be sent to them, it never was.

Chapter 30

WILLARD'S INTOLERANCE OF VEHICULAR IMMOBILITY

Willard had very little patience with a vehicle that failed to operate in the manner he wished. He had one truck which was a staked flat bed... it was a big truck. He had been having trouble getting it started and even more trouble keeping it running. It would just quit at the most inopportune time. It happened to do that one day just out of La Grange, Texas. Harry was fed up. He carried all of the titles to the vehicles with him in a leather pouch. He took out the title, signed it on the back, stuck it under the windshield wiper, and drove off with the rest of the show merrily down the road.

Years later you could drive through La Grange and see one of the city garbage collection trucks with the words, "Willard the Wizard" emblazoned on the side.

Harry's son-in-law, Whitey, told me that there really was not much wrong with the truck. It needed a carburetor cleaning and overhaul, minor adjustments, a new wiring loom, and a general tune up. Harry did not care; that was an end to one more headache.

Chapter 31

MURRAY NEVELS

Murray Nevels always worshipped Harry Willard. He even worked in advance of the Willard show for a while. Later he went into the uniform business. He had all kinds of rental uniforms such as nurses, barbers, beauty salon workers, and eventually branched out into the rental and laundering of linens for restaurants.

Nevels always loved the Goddess and Reptile illusion. I have previously explained my experiences with that particular trick. I guess it would be fair to say that I just flat disliked the mystery. Harry knew how much Nevels loved it and wished for one. During those years, Nevels simply did not have the kind of money it would take to have the Thayer Magic Manufacturing Company build him one. It was an exceedingly difficult piece of stage furniture to construct. Finally Harry said, "Don if you really never intend to do anything with it why don't you give it back to me and I will give it to Murray. I still have a few smaller items around and I will trade you something for it." Since he had already given me the bulk of his stage magic years ago and the rest Johnny Daniels took, I thought it over and told him he had nothing that would benefit me but to take the Goddess anyway. He took it to Murray Nevels. Upon Nevels' death it was really interesting to note that he had either bought or constructed quite a large show--all big illusions. Two garages full; but, from all I could learn, he never performed a single show with it.

It was Murray who helped Willard draft the original "Raggedy Anne" illusion, which I still use... or at least I did use up until my health failed and I could no longer perform. What this did was correct the failing in the tip-over box principle. Let me explain. *(See Appendix B-11)*

In with all of that mountain of equipment Willard gave me, was his "Jack in the Box" or, as he liked to call it, the "Monkey Switch." This was a large tip-over box. Anyone familiar with the principle knows that assistants had better be standing on each side of the box or else the person in and out of the box, can be seen from extreme side angles when it is tipped over because they are crouching behind the box. Well this method eliminates that because the person so hidden is sitting with their back to the flap in the bottom of the box as opposed to it facing them. There is a strap on the flap that is held in the assistants right hand and is just over their right shoulder. So when the box is tipped forward, their body is not a couple of feet or so in back of the box, but rather it is right up against it. Their legs are not visible because the box sits on a platform with beautiful ornate legs acting as a base built like that of a doll house illusion. So it is two illusions in one and it is the only illusion, that I know of, that has the assistant working it BACKWARDS.

The way we do this trick is to show the box part empty. From a drawer box we produce a small Raggedy Ann doll. I offer her to Joyce who rejects her so I drop the doll in the illusion, spin it around, and reach in to take out the doll that has now grown to twice its size... that is repeated and the doll doubles in size each time until finally a live girl dressed as Raggedy Ann emerges.

Chapter 32

THE RETURN OF CARL & JACK

Many legendary people who worked with and for me have drifted in and out of my life... some several times each. Jack Tiger, mentioned earlier, is one. Carl Balmer is another.

Tiger booked the show, both spooks and illusion, during four separate and quite distinct periods of my life. They were with varying degrees of success. Nothing that I ever did with him approached the success we achieved together with the spook operas. Tiger did as well as most with the illusion show, but nothing that he ever did after the ghosts shows approached the success that Carl Balmer had promoting my illusion show. So I guess it was a toss-up between the two. Jack Tiger's calling was with motion picture houses and Balmer's was with auditoriums.

Balmer came back into my life briefly in 1986. We had planned to crank it up again and he seemed to have a plan that would be sure fire. Carl Balmer had found that there is a very large number of old, historic, restored opera houses across the nation. There is even an association of them. He obtained the list and became a member of their association. Each of these theatres has a local support group for fund raising, preservation, etc. Carl decided that those groups would be excellent sponsors. He composed, in his inimitable style, a really fetching letter to solicit such sponsorship. It was his idea to dress the ladies of these support groups in "leg of mutton" sleeve blouses and in the style of the 1800's. It was to be the "Old-Fashioned Opera House Magic Show" with an all out campaign using every known type of direct solicitation for the sale of tickets plus a few new ones. He mailed a couple of dozen of these letters out and was gratified with the replies. We ordered the special printing of brochures, letterheads, letters, sample tickets, and general outlines of what we planned to do for each sponsor. Carl went home to Del Rio, Texas, after spending a week with us in Virginia laying it all out.

The day after he got back to Del Rio, he and Bess decided to go across the border to Villa Acuna and have dinner at Mrs. Crosby's, the most popular eatery in Old Mexico. Before leaving he knocked a wasp's nest down on the front porch. That night after Carl and Bess returned from Villa Acuna, he was watching the Johnny Carson show and Bess had gone to bed. He came in the bedroom and said, "Bess." She replied, "What is it Carl?" He said, "Baby, I think that I am dying." He fell to the floor dead. The autopsy found a wasp stinger where he had been stung. He died from anaphylactic shock and never even knew why. *(See Appendix A-15)*

Jack Tiger was so tremendously talented in the field of promotional show business that one had to overlook his idiosyncrasies. Some said that he was "nuts." No matter--because history demonstrates an overabundance of "detached" individuals. Here is an example of some of Tiger's thinking. When he went into the Marines' they, as was the rule of the day, insisted on giving him a "crew cut" and a shave. He did not like it. In fact he hated it. When he "mustered out" of the service, he vowed that he would never have another shave and/or haircut. HE DIDN'T. It got to the point that when you saw him walking toward you on the street, the vision with which you were greeted was a torso, arms, legs, etc. but on top was a mound of thick, black, kinky, curly hair with only two eyes peering out at you. He looked so bad that his mother and father refused to allow him to attend the wedding of his sister Marion.

Tiger was so overwhelmed with the success of the Gorilla act wherein the audiences would see this giant gorilla at various places all over the theatre, the lights would go out, again and again, only to have the gorilla reappear each time in a different location. Pandemonium broke out among the spectators. These gorilla suits looked terrific. The arms had extensions which gave the appearance of them almost dragging on the floor. When the operator opened his mouth the gorillas mouth opened. The way the suits were made gave the impression of shorter legs and massive chests. Well, Tiger started thinking, my gosh, what if one of the suits gets ruined, stolen, lost, or God only knows what else, and he saw our strongest feature go up in smoke. So he ordered 10 suits. In those days the gorilla outfit ran about $800. Today that would be the equivalent of $8,000. Maybe lurking in the back of his mind was the thought that I would have to eventually put out more units of the show under my name in order to fill all the requests for dates and that he would be one of those unit providers. Anyway we had a very large supply of gorillas.

Willard had a very convenient memory. Let me explain. When he and Gene turned all of the really big stage props over to me, Harry wanted to retain several items. He gave me tons of illusions. Most of this equipment was completed and in good repair. Some illusions even had the costumes with them. Harry only kept his old triple trunks (the canon had long since been lost to time), his doll house, substitution trunk, cabinet, and the small magic. He told me that he would never be able to do the really big shows again. He was right. John Daniel took five items and all the rest became the Brandon show. Mainly, I think, he just wanted things around to look at and remember. He did also hang onto a part of one of his levitations.

In with the magic and illusions Harry gave me, were any number of parts of tricks. In order to repair, or rebuild, these mysteries would require prior knowledge of them and perhaps, their histories. Some of it I have simply never gotten around to doing. Not to this day and that is a shame.

Once while Harry was in the hospital he called me to come and see him. A couple of fellows and I went out and took him some fruit and candy. He was not interested in the things we took him and that should have tipped me off. He got me off to the side and said, "Don, my house car is just standing open. Can you go out and do me a favor?" I told him that I would try. Harry said, "Please take my trunks, leve, sword, doll house, and important stuff and look after it for me until I get out of here."

I did not have a truck at the time and had just suffered a financial loss, from which I am still trying to recover. I did move that which I could in the back of a station wagon. I thought it strange because just a short time earlier I had given Harry about $2,000 worth of items such as a new Marshall blooming bouquet (the large automatic one) a number of production bouquets, a canary in the light bulb, etc. None of that apparatus was to be found. I have always felt that someone had been there and removed some of Harry's things.

What we did not know, at the time, was when Harry whispered to me to secure the items I have mentioned, he was "out of it" because he, amazingly, had been drinking. I registered a complaint against the physician responsible but to no avail. Finally, some time later, after he was released he came to see me mad as hell, and demanded his stuff back and accused me of having stolen two or three things from him. This simply was not true. Even if it were true, he owed me a lot of money. That was not the slightest bit of consequence because Harry did everyone like this... Howard, Rosemary, Gene, Madeline, Frances, etc... he would be looped and tell a person something and then sober up and completely forget it, or vice versa causing a great deal of pain. Personally, it never mattered to me. I simply accepted that facet of his personality and made allowances for it. Others did not. I am sure that some carried a grudge against Willard to their graves. Regardless of any of this, it was just simply impossible not to love the man. There was a quality about Harry Willard that could not be denied. The only word that explains it is charm. He could be the kindest person in the world and in one moment change into the meanest of monsters. Those really close to him just overlooked this because, after all, they were in the company of what was, undoubtedly, the very best magician that ever lived. I did not see Harry during the very last period of his life. I was living a long way off from him, but an interesting set of circumstances was told to me by his daughter Madeline which I plan to relate next.

Harry was in a nursing home and miserable as hell. When Madeline would go to visit him all he could talk about was getting away from that awful place. Finally Madeline, and her husband Bill, gave in and moved Harry to their home. In due course they started missing Harry from around the house. He would just be gone for hours and days. On occasion they would hear noises coming from the garage in the wee hours of the morning. It would be hammering, sawing, bending of metal, etc. and not wishing to pry, Bill and

Madeline could only guess at what was going on.

More time passed, and then one day, Harry came home in a new station wagon. Madeline said that it was one of the funniest things she ever saw. It looked as though Harry was riding a bucking horse. Willard was simply not accustomed to driving an automatic transmission, power steering, and brakes. He had miraculously gone out daily, by bus when necessary, and booked the towns surrounding San Antonio. Places like Fredericksburg, New Braunfels, Seguin, Stockdale, Boerne, etc. Then he proceeded to construct a small show and performed in all of these cities by himself. He earned enough to buy the vehicle and do pretty much as he pleased. At that very late date in his life he proved that it could still be done. Harry and my grandfather were the only two human beings that I ever thought could accomplish something like this. Also the story about alcohol shortening lives... I don't know because both men lived to very ripe old ages. Just goes to show you. Harry Willard died on the 28th of June, 1970.

Chapter 33

HAIR TODAY AND
GONE TOMORROW

Whenever Harry and Pappy took me with them, one or the other would identify me to the waiter or bartender as their son. Even at a very young age I was served alcoholic beverages to drink. I was big for my age by then, and most tavern operators did not seem to care.

There was one exception. I remember Pappy was going southwest of San Antonio to shoe some horses on one of the ranch's and Willard went along because he wanted to stop and try to book a show or two at a couple of high schools. Along the way we stopped at a place called the "Grey Eagle." I cannot remember just where it was located, but I do remember it was at a fork in the road and nothing else near it. It was a big stone building. We went in and Harry and Pappy each ordered a huge glass of beer. They ordered one for me also. The bartender said, "No, this kid's too young". So Harry and Pappy each changed their order to two glasses of beer. With four glasses sitting on the table they each pushed one over in front of me. So I had two glasses and they each had only one. Quickly I downed mine before the bartender saw what was going on. Then I tried to stand up and I fell flat on my fanny. I learned that you just cannot drink that stuff too fast. Pappy did not shoe any horses that day and Willard did not book any shows.

Willard wore a fake goatee and moustache on stage. After a while I did, too. To look even older I whitened my hair. That is I put white make-up at the temples and the sides, but I left it brown on top. After a while I thought it might be an altogether good idea if it were all white so I bleached the top. A little later I found that the sides no longer needed make-up. They had turned white. Then the top of my head turned white also. No more lightener or make-up was needed. Then my hair started coming out on top. As I grew balder I learned to live with it. All of those that have had hair replacement and/or transplantation look super fakey to me. It never looks natural.

At first, I only wore a glue-on goatee. Later, I started gluing on a moustache. Then I found that it looked better if I simply drew the moustache on, each day, with an eyebrow pencil. Then I abandoned all of it and let my moustache grow; the same applied to the goatee. They looked alright as long as they were dark. Then the goatee and moustache turned white also. I do not particularly like it but I am stuck with it. I think the original sticking it on and being able to take it off after the last show at night, came from Willard's double identity thesis. I guess I wanted to copy him. Later, I realized this duo personality of his went much deeper--that was the main deciding factor. I think it is true about balding that bald people really do not think of themselves as bald and that it is everyone else who is just hairy.

Chapter 34

UNCLE ED

History seems to be checkered with magicians who presented a true Mephistolean appearance. Not the least of whom was Willard. However, I believe that Harry was the only one that carried, with the Devilish look, the added mirthful overtones. He could give an audience a look, a stare, a raised eyebrow that simply brought on a roar of laughter. It took me a long time to come to the full realization that his being able to provoke gales of laughter was entirely contrived. It was something that he would actually stand in front of a mirror and practice. He, in the course of a performance, seemingly caused something magical to happen that both startled and bemused himself as well as those watching. He could cause an eyebrow to shoot up almost to his hairline.

Harry was a great one for using ladies undergarments during a show. He would manage to produce a brassiere with three (3) cups. He would have one of the volunteers during the hypnotic demonstration put on panties, bras, corsets, slips, etc... when he did this he always managed to find a male subject that was slightly obese and he made sure that the ladies things were sizes too small to fit properly on that man. Before he commenced this display he would always ask the subject if he (subject) believed in hypnotism, had ever been hypnotized, would allow it to be tried, etc. If the subject said "no," it made it all the funnier because when he would awaken the man from the trance and the subject looked down and saw what he was wearing, he would frequently run up the aisle embarrassed.

I have always wondered why audiences, both men and women, seem to find those items of female clothing, that is normally hidden from view, so very funny. Even tiny children think they are hilarious. It does seem to be a perpetual absurdity.

When my grandfather had his shop across from our grocery store and meat market, my Aunt Drussie (Drucilla) and Uncle Ed McAda had a small ice house and convenience store up at the corner two doors away. They were wonderful people. Never a hostile word passed their lips concerning anyone. Uncle Ed however, as do most other people I have known, had a "peculiarity." He was a member of a strange cult. He did call it a "religion" but it was unlike anything I ever heard of either before or since. They were called the "money hunters."

These "money hunters" had another name for their religion but I have forgotten what it was. They had a limb off of a tree, with a fork in it that was very much like the "divining rods" used by those who claim to be able to locate underground water for well diggers. They would walk around with the point end of the limb sticking out ahead of them and when that limb dipped a little bit downward, they would claim that was the location of buried money.

The very first time my grandfather took me to see the "Willard the Wizard" show, my entire family attended. It was my mother, my grandmother, my uncle, my grand uncle, and my great aunt. My Uncle Ed was very much taken by Willard, and in particular, his spirit cabinet and ghost tricks. After the performance, my grandfather introduced Uncle Ed to Willard. After that, whenever Willard was in the store or over at my grandfather's shop, here would come Uncle Ed. He and some of the other "money hunters' pestered Harry with great consistency... they kept trying to talk Willard into going out with them on one of their money hunting expeditions. I believe that they must have decided that Willard had some sort of occult powers and that he could lead them to the money. Finally Harry gave in and agreed to go with them one night to an old abandoned graveyard, way south of San Antonio. Harry later told us it was one of the most extraordinary experiences of his life. These money hunters would all, both men and women, get down on their knees and pray, in the moonlight, for divine guidance in locating the buried money. They would walk around with the forked limb and several of them would each be touching the limb. The limb would dip and there the "hunters" would dig. This went on for hours. Harry was tired. He had a bleeding tongue from biting it in order to keep from laughing out loud. Harry knew that the dipping of the limb had nothing to do with divinity but the mere fact that the limb was heavy and the "hunter's" arms got tired would precipitate a slight dip. Harry had enough of this nonsense and asked them to give him the magic limb. He walked around several of the old tombstones and sure enough the limb dipped. They dug and believe it or not, they found a large coin... then another. They were convinced that they were on the right track with Willard. Harry would have humored them longer if only he had not run out of whiskey. He carried a silver flask in his right back pocket. It was just enough for two drinks so you can well imagine that it did not last very long.

Willard always carried two silver dollars in his pocket for a very specific reason which I intend to explain very shortly.

Often a local fire inspector would corner Willard, and in effect, ask if the scenery, curtains, and costumes were fireproof. This was silly because in those days there was absolutely no such thing as fireproofing. There were certain substances which alledged to be "flame retardant," but I even harbor doubts about them. When an "inspector" would make such inquires of Willard there was an interesting way Harry had of dealing with them. He would first take a couple of large, black Havana cigars from his pocket and give one to the inspector. Harry would light one for himself. He would keep puffing on that cigar until the tip glowed with that reddish orange which demonstrated great heat. Then Harry would take the inspector by the arm, over to a curtain and gather part of it between his thumb and fingers on the left hand. He would then take the cigar and slowly grind it into the curtain and brush away the ashes revealing the curtain completely unharmed. He accomplished this by palming (hiding in his hand) one of the silver dollars which he slipped under the curtain without the knowledge of the fire inspector. The metal dollar gave him a very firm base upon which to slowly extinguish the burning end of the cigar. It all looked very convincing and the inspector usually went away satisfied. On occasion, an inspector would simply and blatantly come with his hand out wanting a "pay off." Harry did pay some of these people off.

It was these two silver dollars which Willard dropped into the open "dig," pushed them under the earth with his shovel, and let the "money hunters" find. Like a child on an Easter egg hunt. The "hunters" almost worried him to death because now, don't you see, they were convinced that Willard was put on this earth for the sole purpose of helping them locate buried money. He really had great difficulty convincing them otherwise. Finally after one of his trips to the hospital he told them that he had lost all of his magic powers but if they ever returned he would immediately let the "hunters" know about it. He never did.

Willard's compulsive vitality was always accompanied by a slight influence of chicanery. Like Barnum he sort of clung to a degree of humbug. Just as in the fire inspectors situations, he outwitted most of them.

Willard's learning activities with his father were obviously didactic; but his ability with hand and power tools, inventiveness, ability to create new ways of doing old things including manipulation happened to be, I think, entirely autodactic. He did display great powers of reason and logic when it came to others. The problem seemed to be in applying those powers to himself. Case in point, when the motion picture houses raised their prices from 15¢ admission Harry went on charging the same. Then the theatres went to 25¢ and Harry charged15¢. When the houses charged 35¢, Harry was furious. He thought it should be some sort of a crime to charge people that outrageous amount to see any show... Finally when movies were a dollar and he was still charging 50¢, it dawned on him that the theatre staff was miniscule compared to his; and he did admit, reluctantly, that maybe he had not been charging enough all along.

My Uncle Ed was a great "whittler." He could carve most anything. Once he made me a tiny box that looked like a small orange crate with slat sides and a round ball inside the box. Yet it was all carved out of one piece of wood. How on earth he managed to carve that little ball inside the little crate I do not know.

Willard had great carving abilities in common with Uncle Ed. Willard carved all of his puppets, made their little clothes, painted them, strung them, etc. I do not think that anyone would have that much patience today.

Anyone familiar with white tie and tails (full dress clawhammer coat) knows that the stiff front shirt that is worn with such apparel has a detachable collar. These collars are very stiffly starched. They have a button in back of the neck and then they button in front. Harry had boxes full of these collars. He would change them sometimes, several times a day. He did not always keep track of the clean supply. I have seen him run out of the collars and simply take a piece of white cardboard, like those used inside a new shirt, draw around a dirty collar, cut it out with a pair of scissors, and then put it on to wear. From just a couple of feet it was impossible to tell the difference. Just one of his thousands of ingenuities.

Chapter 35

POLITICAL CORRECTNESS
AND ILLUSIONISTS

With the many and strange differing political viewpoints of today, it seems to me that the term, "political correctness," is a dichotomy. At best it is a simple contradiction in terms. Who dares allege that his opinion of what is, or is not, correct politically, in so far as the many diverse ideologies are concerned. Who can, with a straight face, proclaim that he speaks for all... The whole notion seems to me to be an absurdity. Nevertheless some have managed to attack the illusionists who still use female assistants. These antagonists claim that the relationship between the illusionist and his female assistant is that of the sado-masochist.

Some feminists complain that the male illusionists frequently use women in devices that represent sawing the female in half, cutting them into thirds, fourths, fifths, sixths, hanging, decapitating, crushing, stretching, burning, piercing, and just about every other tortuous mechanism imaginable. What those who criticize fail to mention is that in every single case, of which I am aware, the lady emerges unscathed and triumphant at the end of the trick. More importantly, I think, the female is generally smaller, more petite, more supple, better suited, and prettier than the male. They are simply able to fit into smaller places, tricks, hidden compartments, than men and even boys. Still, today, a number of illusionists have switched over to using males in their illusions instead of women.

Harry Willard had an interlude in one of his shows that was so pretty, appealing, and novel that it would probably be met with success today. It is something that must be seen in person and would prove to be valueless in a motion picture or on television. Let me tell you about it. The curtain would open on a dark stage. Suddenly a beautiful picture would appear on a screen center stage. Let us say that the first scene would be among the cherry blossoms and a lovely girl in oriental dress with a bamboo parasol standing in the middle. This scene would evolve out of what originally was a myriad of bleeding colors that seemed to blend together to create the picture. The next thing that the audience would notice was that the scene was not "flat," but rather three dimensional. Just when the audience started thinking that the girl was really a manikin, she would smile and the colors would start bleeding again and rearrange themselves in an altogether different scene. The next picture might be a young woman in Holland with the dikes, windmills, wooden shoes, and interesting dress. Once again she would smile and the visible image would alter itself into something completely different. It usually concluded with the American flag as the background and the Statue of Liberty in the middle; and then the lady would, again, smile. It was not until this juncture that the lights would come up and the audience would see that the lady, standing on a snow white stool, was just dressed in a white robe and standing in front of a white curtain. This was accomplished with duo slide projectors and a unique mechanism which allowed for the "unfocusing" of the picture while one side of the machine was dimming and the other side brightening. The colors seemed to run together and create a kaleidoscopic view while the transformation took place. The complication in the creation of the act was in the photographing of each scene because the subject had to remain in the exact same place and the camera could not be moved either. This simply meant that the lady would have to put on one of the costumes while the background and set pieces were being placed around her. The picture had to be properly lit. When the photo was taken the woman had to change her costumes and resume that exact same position for the shooting of the next scene. After these 35 mm transparencies had been developed, the face of the woman had to be carefully, painstakingly etched out. In actual performance, the entire picture was projected on her and the curtain. Her real face would show through but all else would be projected photographic imagery. Prior to each performance, great care was taken to insure that the projection equipment was located in the very same position. Markings on the stage placed the subject in her clearly defined space, as well. The act was known as the "Plastique Poses." Should this novelty ever be re-created, I am sure that it will be met with criticisms from some who will undoubtedly claim that it imposes a very difficult physical requirement on the woman and great stress simply because the subject would have to stand in the very same position for such a long time. Still it really did look neat.

Chapter 36

DRUM BEATERS

In the period prior to the '60's, we had a large number of professional publicists and agents that went out and booked a tour or an entire season. Then this person would go back and wait until about one week to 10 days before the show was to commence the tour. Whereupon the person would go ahead of the show, and like the "barker" in a side show, extolled the virtues and greatness of the coming theatrical attraction. These people were, colorful, flamboyant, gregarious, and very knowledgeable. Newspaper editors looked forward to their coming because they brightened the days with interesting stories to tell. Editors would always, be glad to give some "free" space to the attraction, and often, to the drumbeater himself. These news stories did not cost the show anything and were viewed as an informative public service. Stories would include photos of the show. Each release was designed to peak the curiosity of the potential patron. Shows could be "sold" to the public by the stories reducing the need for outdoor advertising (posters) and ad space in the newspaper which the show had to pay for. A great "drum beater" could make, or break, a show. They were surely worth their weight in gold. They are all gone now with the possible exception of John McConnell. John has been out with just about every show of note today. Not just the circuses but theatrical style roadshows. He

136

successfully pulled the Hanneford Circus out and made it into the number one Shrine Circus in America today. John is thoroughly familiar with every phase of showbusiness. He is also a magician of note and a great humanitarian combined. During the years that John McConnell was the general manager of the Big Apple Circus, that show sailed to heights that no one would ever have imagined.

John McConnell is a tall handsome man. He is a specialist in psychology, business, showbusiness, some law, public relations, advertising, and an exotic knowledge of how to make things work. His McConnell and Simmons Company was responsible for "pulling the fat out of the fire" for some of America's better known industries. John could take any show of merit, even today, and put it on the very top. I had hoped that his son Eric would follow in his footsteps. If not Eric, the other son Brian. Apparently, neither will do so. It is a shame because when John is gone I do not think there will be another.

Chapter 37

LUNA BELTS

A lady brought a little boy to see me one day and he asked me if it is true that magicians can fly. I explained to the child that magicians are all notorious liars. Just about everything they do is a lie. It is done for entertainment and that purpose only. There is no such thing as a magician, only actors playing the part of what they think a magician should be like. Still it kind of bothers me that some children today are thinking that there are people who have genuine magical powers. I do think this to be something that could result in a disaster. I always issue a disclaimer on this. In the legal climate of our era, I expect to see a huge lawsuit for damages arising out of just such an occurrence.

I guess that the flying thing goes back to the original "Luna Belt" that was used to produce an illusion wherein a lady walks out on the stage on one side and then, effortlessly, takes a step that lands her clear across the stage on the opposite side. This harness has been used, in various forms, by people like Mary Martin and Sandy Duncan in "Peter Pan," Julie Andrews in "Mary Poppins" and numerous others.

You would almost have to see one in order to understand and appreciate the really fine machine work that goes into it. It is a steel belt within another slightly larger steel belt. Between the two are a series of roller type bearings that operate in a track which encircles the body. In other words, one belt (the inner one) can spin inside the outer one. Then on each side is a knob-like affair to which attach the wires that allow for the rising and lowering. Each knob has a bearing in it that will allow the person wearing the contrivance to turn head over heals, in rotation and at the same time spin, if she so desires, inside the belt. There is a strap that goes between the person's legs for support. The wires that were used were the fine music wire; and if it were the chromed variety, the shining appearance had to be subdued before performances by spraying the wire with vinegar, causing a rusty appearance. This dull surface of the wire made it virtually invisible in proper lighting. A wire on each side at the knob goes up into the "catwalk" above the stage where the whole thing can travel back and forth, on a track. By raising or lowering the person that is "flying" and moving the set of wires across the stage horizontally, you have the appearance of the subject stepping up into the air and floating about all over the stage. They can spin, make strange gyrations, somersaults, or just lie there in mid air. Today they have developed a method whereby the two supporting wires can separate and travel in opposite directions on the track and even come down the walls of the stage behind the wing curtains. Then the person "flying" can seemingly be sleeping in the air and held in place by almost horizontal wires which allow for hoops to be passed over and even encircle the floating subject repeatedly.

It is a startling effect when properly presented, but certainly should never impart to anyone (child or adult) that a human being can really fly.

Willard had several of the "Luna Belts," but I do not remember whatever happened to them.

Chapter 38

WILLARD'S CALLIOPE DAZE

Sometimes I think the single possession of which Willard was the most fond, was his steam calliope. This was a magnificent musical instrument rarely, if ever, seen today. In a sense it is like a pipe organ. The sound comes from a series of pipes produced by steam passing through them. There are keys to be pushed just like an organ, piano, accordion, etc. The Willard steam calliope was a wondrous sight to behold. Painted a little more sedately than those used by circus companies of the time but the gold, blue, green, red, yellow, and complimentary colors were tastefully applied in such a manner as to make it well worth just viewing what could make all that racket.

The calliope could be heard for miles. In smaller towns the whole population was treated to its annoyance. Willard wanted the calliope played upon the arrival of the show in town. Later, he wanted it played again to let everyone know that the show was unloaded and being set up for the performance that was to take place that same evening. Finally the calliope was played about a half hour before the ticket wagon was opened for business. That business was the selling of the best seats in the house, those closest to the stage, and that those tickets promised to take the ticketholder on a "magic carpet" journey into a land of fantasy beyond imagination.

Townspeople knew of the calliope and its connection with the

Willard show. They had come to expect it over the years. What they did not expect were some of the outrageous things that Willard did with the steam instrument.

Occasionally when Willard would come in after having sampled a "wee bit too much" of his favorite beverages. Often in the very early hours of the morning Willard would fire up the calliope. When he finally had a full head of steam he would start pushing on the keys. Harry was NOT a musician. He just seemed to like the noise. The more he drank, the more he must have thought that he was a full symphony orchestra... at least until such time as the police arrived.

After the last fire, Willard sold the calliope. I do not know who bought it. If it still exists... God... I wish I could see it again.

Chapter 39

TIJAHNY

The only thing in recent times which could even be considered to start to approach the vastness of the tented theatre of Willard would be the Tijahny Show which came up out of Mexico. From what I understand Tijahny is not from Mexico or South America. Rumor has it that he immigrated from one of the Balkan countries. He did manage to learn to speak Spanish fluently and enjoyed the very best of successes in the Spanish speaking countries. The Tijahny Show carried a huge tented theatre with a theatrical end and a full stage equipped for every possible scenic display, lighting, sound, curtains, etc. The scenic beauty of this show cannot be denied. The costumes were a cross between the Ziegfield and Las Vegas styles. The chorus line reminded one of the Radio City Music Hall's "Rockets." The magical props were excellent in appearance and performed flawlessly. The show died in America.

Why? What could have gone wrong? This beautiful "glitzy" show, following the line of current thinking, should have, by all accounts, been a great success. Maybe I can provide some clues. I must go back to something Willard told me a long, long time ago. He said, "Until the time comes that you can go out on a stage, stand there, and keep the audience spellbound with your voice alone for at least an hour and a half, you should not even consider trying to entertain them with a trick." With all the beautiful, sexy, wonderfully costumed women and gorgeous sets behind him why did the beautiful magic of Tijahny fail? Why could a tired old man walk out in front of an audience of 3,000, uncoil a piece of hemp cord (packing box rope) a quarter of an inch in diameter and bring that huge audience to their feet in one of the longest sustained ovations ever? This Willard did consistently.

There were many shows of magic in Mexico and South America. Justinanni, Fong Tu Yeen, Professor Alba, Paco Miller, Fu Manchu (David Bamberg), and others. These shows, while successful in their own countries just could not make it in America. Paco Miller was every bit as good as Edger Bergen and when he threw his voice the audience saw no movement of the thyroid or lip area. His show followed many of the precepts laid down by Willard and was astonishingly successful. Not in America.

In analyzing the persona of Willard and Harry Blackstone, Sr., there was only thing which set them apart from the others. It was not the magic. A fellow by the name of George Marquis came close; so did John Calvert. The rest only yearned for it. What quality is so missing in others? How could they make audiences fall in love with them like some movie stars such as Bing Crosby, Al Jolson, Jimmy Durante, and so many more? Not particularly beautiful people. Still they were revered... almost worshipped. Why do people, even today, who saw these entertainers remember them, right now, as though it were yesterday? Betcha they will not be able to say that about Sigfried and Roy, Melinda, Lance Burton, David Copperfield, and yes, even Blackstone, Jr. Please do not misunderstand me; Harry Blackstone, Jr. presents one of the finest magic and illusion shows ever. He has a beautifully rich, well-projected voice. It is not his father's voice. If he had his father's voice he would reach the epitome, the pinnacle of success that neither he, nor his father, ever even dreamed. Not necessarily a pretty voice; sometimes almost metallic and raspy, but one that you will never forget. Harry Willard and Harry Blackstone, Sr. had voices which were almost identical. If you put each in a room and stood outside the closed door you probably would not be able to say, for sure, which man was talking. That was the real secret of their success as entertainers. As in the case of Frank Sinatra, "THE VOICE."

143

Tom Liberto lived in San Antonio, Texas. His daughter Vivian was the first wife of the country and western singer Johnny Cash. Tom's son Raymond was also a singer. He had one hit record, it was "Wild, Wild Woman." After that I heard no more of him. Tom Liberto owned an insurance Agency in San Antonio. He was a great fan of magic and a capable close up magician himself. He booked Aldo Richardi, Jr. into the National Theatre for two weeks. This was Richardi's first trek in the U.S., but that two weeks ran over into six weeks because of public demand. Richardi had a very good singing voice and he danced well. He performed his magic and illusions like a ballet dancer perhaps would. A better magic show, as such, I have never seen. Even with his appearances on the Ed Sullivan "Toast of the Town" weekly television show, Richardi never attained the recognition that was probably due him. Why? Once again, the voice.

Chapter 40

FLOWERS IN THE SNOW

In our show, for many years, one of the opening tricks was the mysterious production of copious quantities of beautifully-colored flowers from an empty cone of paper. This trick was originated by De Kolta and carried to its greatest height by Willard. Female assistants would stand on stage with large open bubble-type parasols held upside down. The magician picks up a sheet of cartridge paper (poster or menu board) and after having shown it fairly on each side, rolls the paper into a cone. A clothespin holds the cone in that position. Again the interior of the cone is displayed in such a manner as to demonstrate that it is truly empty. Whereupon the cone suddenly fills itself with an overflowing quantity of lovely, varied colored flowers. The magician starts pouring these flowers out of the cone into one of the upturned parasols. He continues to pour flowers until the parasol is filled to its brim and starts to spill over. The magician then turns to the next parasol and fills it, and so on. Audiences love this trick.

This is accomplished by two things. First is the actual construction of the flower itself. It is made with a spring inside which causes it to open when released from confinement, otherwise it is perfectly flat. Large quantities of these flowers can be concealed in a very small space. They are packaged in bundles and hidden in various places on the magician's person and elsewhere about the stage.

Getting each bundle into the cone and then popping the release is the really tricky part. So secondly, the entertainer must distract the audience's vision each time a new bundle of the flowers is introduced into the cone. This is done in many different ways. An overflowing flower falls to the floor and the gaze of the spectators follows the falling flowers. A girl opening one of the other parasols, etc. Each time a new group of flowers must be secretly placed in the cone, there is a coverup.

Regardless of how assiduously the flowers are handled and cared for, they are delicate and can easily be destroyed. We used 1,500 of the flowers. Joyce, my wife, always carried the flowers in a gunmetal grey money box that was about 10" wide, 12" long, and three inches thick.

We were staying in a motel on the interstate near Fort Worth, Texas, enroute to Arkansas and the money box of flowers was on the front seat. It was very cold and had snowed about three inches during the night. A thief broke into our truck and took my wife's new coat, a gun, and the money box. I am sure that he was convinced he had come upon the "find" of a lifetime and that the box was filled with money. He probably could not wait to find refuge, away from the motel, where he could break the money box open and manage to get his hands on all that money. He must have hurried across the highway, which was a cloverleaf, and down the side of a hill. He stopped and took a large rock and broke open the lock, which was really frail. Boy, can't you just see him when he was suddenly covered fanny deep in those flowers! I would be willing to bet that he thought twice after that when breaking something open.

The next morning, after discovering our loss, we decided to drive around and look for evidence for our insurance company. As we made the turn on the cloverleaf we were greeted by the sight of a myriad of color sprinkled throughout the snow. The sight of all those beautiful flowers in that background of white was startling to say the least.

On the subject of misdirecting the audience, I think that the very most impressive display of that was on the McDonald Birch Show. Birch would be standing in the center of the stage holding the little bunny which he had just taken out of the nest of boxes. The bunny was wearing a borrowed wristwatch tied around its neck with

146

a ribbon. As birch stood there, Pat Paterson would come walking out onstage with his left hand held open, palm up, at waist height. Sitting on his left hand was about a #16 brown paper bag--opened. On the backside of the bag was Paterson's right hand, out of sight, steadying the bag. As Pat approached Birch, the magician would turn to face Pat with his right side to the audience. Birch would take the bunny in his left hand and drop him into the paper bag, and in a single movement, take the bag off of Paterson's hand and walk out to the footlight and simply crush it. He would toss the crushed bag offstage. The bunny was gone.

What really happened was that the bag had a rather large hole cut in it backside which the audience never saw. Paterson had his right hand inside the bag and not on the outside as everyone assumed. When Birch dropped the bunny into the bag that rabbit went directly into Paterson's hand and was instantly withdrawn from the backside and held down at Paterson's right side just above the knee. Paterson just kept walking. All eyes remained on Birch and the bag. It was startling and very effective. Birch told me that no one ever caught him doing it. One time he did have a rabbit that really was very wild and simply went crazy and jumped out of Paterson's hand. The rabbit was loose and running all over the stage but the people viewing the spectacle still did not know where the rabbit came from. Everyone could only remember seeing the rabbit go into the bag and suddenly disappear. Then another bunny appeared running around the stage. No one knew where the "last" bunny came from but it must have been magic.

Chapter 41

VIRGIL AND WILLARD

The Great Virgil (Virgil Mulkey) idolized Willard. Virgil always wanted Willard to teach him how to do Willard's Thumb Tie. Harry told him that if he thought, even for an instant, that he could do it, he would teach it to him right that moment. That was true. Many have attempted to explain how Willard did this trick but none has ever come close. The way Willard presented this trick is the nearest thing, I believe, that audiences will ever see to real magic.

Virgil is the one that gave Willard the ocelot which scratched him up so badly. I always wondered if Virgil really knew just how mean that cat was, and if he did, did he warn Harry about it.

Willard was fond of Virgil but as he would walk away from him, he would say "that big farmer." Harry always made it clear how he felt about those around him as he muttered, under his breath. He always had two opinions of everyone including his own family.

Virgil had a wonderful version of the trick that is known as the "Artist's Dream." This is an open easel affair which allows for a clear view beneath, behind, and all around the easel. A rectangular wooden frame covered with white "newstock" paper is hung on the front of the easel. The magician pops through the paper and produces large amounts of lovely colored silk scarves, and finally, a girl comes bursting through the paper. Although there appears to be no place for

148

concealment and the assistants, as well as the magician, can walk all the way around it, obviously the girl and silk scarves are hidden. This is how.

The lower one third of the easel is an attractive lattice work affair that can be seen through. Behind the lattice work is a flat suspended platform that is black and matches the background. The girl is on the platform. A flat black roller blind had been pulled up in front of the girl. When a release is tripped, the roller blind rolls itself up and the audience can see beneath the easel; but, when it is extended in front of the girl, she is hidden. She is in that position in the beginning. Then the paper-covered frame is hung in the top of the easel. When this is done, she climbs up in back of the paper. The roller blind is released and the whole thing can be viewed beneath the frame of paper. She is in place to conclude the illusion. Willard wanted it; Virgil made him one. Willard never used it. I have it.

Chapter 42

A PECULIAR DUCK

Our show is a small traveling menagerie. We always carry rabbits, doves, ducks, dogs, cats and from time to time, various and sundry other creatures.

Our very favorite, outside of the dogs and cats, are the ducks. We do not think of the dogs and cats as animals, but more like people and are treated as such.

We love the ducks. They are cute and fun. We had one duck in particular that always "killed" an audience. Naturally we called him Donald. Let me tell you what he did. In every trick in which we used him to magically appear, such as the duck tub, Donald would leap down onto the stage proper and walk calmly out to the footlights and stand there and bow. He would keep bowing until such time as he elicited the proper amount of applause. When the applause subsided he would turn to his left and walk off the stage and go into his cage. There he would remain throughout the balance of the show. People just loved "Donald." They would come back after a performance and ask us how we were able to train "Donald" to do his bows. We would always tell them that we did not figure it out ourselves. We always carried our own footlight troughs and dimmer board. Finally we played an auditorium which had the "tree" lights on the poles out on each side of the auditorium which were rigged to take the place of footlights. We decided to try that lighting out and not use our own. For the first time Donald did NOT do his bow. Then we found his secret. When he was first magically produced he would see the bright footlights and walk down to them. He would stop because of the heat emanating from the footlights. He would stand there and start pecking at the lights. To the audience it looked just as though he was talking his bows. He also knew that his cage would always be found in the same place behind the left wing curtain and there would be food and water located there. Failing in his attempt to "eat" the lights he would go to his cage for a little repast. To him it was all perfectly natural... to us it was something of a small miracle.

While on the subject of peculiar ducks, let me tell you about our dear friend Bill Martin. Bill is also known as "Karlton the Magician." He is a wonderful magician. He is an illusionist of both the old school and the new. He is much more than that. Bill is a personification of show business. He has a vast and extensive knowledge of all phases of theatrics. He is also the producer, director, owner, and general everything for his ice shows. "Karlton's Fantasy on Ice" has existed as several units at a time and played places like the State Fair of Florida for several years running. He has toured all over with his ice shows as well as with his "Magic World of Karlton." Both productions are excellent. He is also a juggler, slack wire walker, actor, publicist, computer genius, agent, costume designer, and too many other things to mention. He is also, like all of us, a little crazy.

Martin builds exceptional illusions and props. He is straight-forward, light-hearted, kind, childish at times, very intelligent, and will not eat properly. Never has. He only wanted to eat french fries and hamburgers. He NEVER ate any vegetables. I think that he would die first. He did branch out to some of the Italian foods and fried chicken with mashed potatoes; but his favorite food is salt bagels and peanut butter. He swears that he would prefer to live on that.

I think that Bill Martin literally wrote the book on the subject of procrastination. He will most always "put off until tomorrow what he could do today." One time he concluded a tour with another show and he had taken his trunk full of props to the railroad station. While waiting for the train to come to take him home to Virginia, he decided to take a nap on top of his trunk. The train came. Everyone tried to

151

convince Bill that he had to get up, see that his trunk was loaded on the train, and board himself. He decided that he would rather continue his nap because, after all, there would always be another train coming along tomorrow.

Martin did work on the Phillip Morris Ghost Show. He would dress up like Frankenstein's Monster and go out on the stage and juggle bones. The horrified audience thought them to be real human bones.

He did not like to smile. I think that he must have thought that if a stone face was good enough for Ed Sullivan that it should work for him. I raised enough hell with him to convince him to smile... sort of. I threatened to kill him if he did not grin. He must not have believed me because such smiles were few and far between. Finally I told him to just always imagine me sitting out in the audience at each of his performances completely naked. That did it. He must have found the smiles were worth the effort because he does it much more now.

I will always number Bill Martin among my closest, dearest friends. He may be the only one... the rest are dying off.

Martin took a really big magic show into the malls. I think he was the first to do this on such a grand scale. He even did a version of the "Aga Levitation" in the shopping malls. He played all over the country with this show and to great success. The fact that he repeated so many of the dates bespeaks the value of the show. *(See Appendix A-16)*

In the social/sexual climate of the day, I imagine that most shows must reveal as much of the female anatomy as the law will allow. Karlton is no exception. Recently he showed me the costumes for his coming season. A woman just wearing a hairpin would be more fully dressed. Honestly... everyone is familiar with the "string bikini" but these costumes almost omit the strings. I asked Karlton if the female skaters objected to wearing such scanty outfits. Karlton inferred that the skaters seemed eager to do so.

It might well be that the success of the ice show is due more to the almost nude skaters than to their skating abilities. At least that could be true in so far as the male audience is concerned. I am sure that most men in the seats are ecstatic.

Bill (Karlton) Martin has, pretty much, cornered the market

when it comes to the plastic ice that is used for the "iceless" ice shows. It is my understanding that these sections of imitation ice are no longer being manufactured. Martin bought all the plastic that was available. Now if anyone wants to produce an "iceless" ice show they come to him to rent the plastic. The sections of the plastic fit together like a jigsaw puzzle. A lady in Florida rented a rink from Martin. She never paid him and she ran off to Europe. Therefore I conclude that some people will do most anything in order to gain possession of some of that plastic.

Everyone that knows Bill Martin speaks of his humaneness. Martin has done so very much for show business and showpeople and he is the very first to always champion their cause; so I have always considered it an honor to help him when and if I can. If one of his shows, either magic or ice, comes your way please do not miss it.

Martin and I have another mutual friend whose name is Elmer Deffenbaugh. *(See Appendix A-17)* Elmer's stage name is "Russell the Magician." Elmer is a pharmacologist at the Medical College of Virginia, but I have not the slightest doubt that he could have done well as a magician/comedian. I have always admired his hilarious magical presentations in act format. When he retires from the College, I hope he will do something of a professional nature in entertainment because the world needs more of his brand of laughs.

All of the old "scare" campaigns still work today just as well as they did in the '40's, '50's, and even back in the '30's. The difference being that there are not enough houses (theatres that are equipped) to handle the show. Newer laws impose severe restrictions that in most instances, rule out the complete darkening of a theatre for the "ghost seance." Without that the ghost show has little value. Kent Cummins of Austin, Texas, figured a way around that problem when I played the University of Texas in 1983. Still modern day America cannot provide the number of theatres in a town that are owned by the same company to make "in house" advertising work on a super saturation campaign. Having our posters in most every theatre in a town, our screen advertisements running to cross-plug the coming of our attraction and an aggressive ticket sale being conducted in all of the theatres several weeks in advance was what insured success. The theatre managers would, very often, have special ticket booths erected over the regular ones. These booths had pictures of the show and the

153

monsters, ghosts, ghouls, vampires, etc. on a scary screen. Every theatre gave out our "faint checks." Everyone in town was well aware of the show's appearance.

In order to accomplish the same thing today it is necessary to go into a city with a minimum of $20,000 in advance to spend on newspaper ads, television commercials, and flooding the town with printed material. That $20,000 must be spent before the first ticket is sold. So it is a gamble. Never forget that the performance dates might bring earthquakes, downpours, snow, inclimate weather or what not. A few such losses can wipe out a small company.

I started thinking that there was only one other "captive" audience that could almost literally be forced to view the advertising in advance of a show at a reasonably low cost. That would be in the high schools. How could such a thing be done on a mass basis? What could possibly pull them together in such a way as to make the booking of a promotion possible and still charge unheard of admission prices? Schools were used to paying no more that 50¢ for their assembly programs and evening shows such as school-produced dramas, band concerts, etc., generally charged only $1.

A friend by the name of Sheldon Bergum and my step son, Kenneth, came up with the answer. Only in-house sponsors that had a national, regional, or state base could manage such a thing. So we set about wooing the various student council associations. Bergum arranged for us to be the co-features of the 1978 National Convention of the Southern Association of Student Councils. The other co-feature was Ronald Reagan. Of the 22 states represented, every single school, without exception, signed up to bring our show to their respective schools.

Not only did the various councils agree to arrange to bring our show to their cities they also would arrange to have us appear in an assembly (preview) show at each of the other schools in their town. That way we earned enough money from these daytime performances to cover all of our expenses and what we earned from the public "Ghost Show" performances in the evening was gravy.

With the help of state association officials we played all over Texas, Oklahoma, Arkansas, Missouri, Tennessee, Virginia, and North Carolina. I owe a special debt of thanks to James Van Stavern of Texas, Ron Andres, and Bob Wall of Arkansas, James Ronald

Murray, and Clarence Lowe of Tennessee, Rick West of Virginia and so many others that I cannot list them. We had requests from all over--thousands of them. Far too many to play and way too far to travel. We enjoyed the same response and numbers as in days of the spook shows in the theatres.

My health started to fail and I simply could not stand up to the rigor of the road as in previous times.

My stepson, Kenneth, looked like he should be a movie star. Girls went crazy over him and bunches were always waiting at the stage door for glimpses of him. Ken is very intelligent and can, truthfully, do just about anything he sets his mind to. After the season was booked he would double back and join the show and travel with us. It seemed as though he were made for it. I have actually seen him walk a steel beam, high above stage floors, and do it like a tight rope walker so he could hang rigging for scenery and illusions. He would do this without ladders. He writes very well. As a booking agent he was fabulous. I actually saw him go out and book six contracts in a single day.

Around the show he was a genuine heart throb for the girls. Scores of young ladies would come back afterward screaming, "Where is Kanny?" He did become disenchanted with the business and turned to building and contracting, which he dearly loves, and does very well. In a way I know how Willard felt when his boys were unwilling to try and follow in his footsteps. I think that maybe I had hoped that my son Don, Jr., or Ken, would have taken over the show; however, the last thing on earth I would ever try to do would be to push, or influence, them in that direction.

We did establish that the basic premise of the ghost shows, properly done, appeal to mass audiences today just as they did way back then. I guess people will always love the idea of being frightened. Contrary to popular belief, fear, in certain forms, can be fun. This certainly explains roller coaster rides and haunted houses in theme parks. The success of such recent motion pictures as the newest version of Dracula underscores this thesis.

One time while we were playing an old vaudeville house in the mid seventies Ken came up with the bright idea of putting on one of the gorilla suits and climbing up the side of the theatre building. The building was several stories tall. On about the sixth floor he was swinging away and we had called the television station and newspaper in order to try and garner some free coverage. Well, as you can probably guess, it did not work out that way. A lady in one of the neighboring office buildings just happened to be looking out one of the windows and saw this gorilla hanging from the roof of the theatre. She called the police and excitedly told them that some sort of an escaped ape (or something) was loose and swinging around on the top of the theatre building. The police came, people from the local zoo came, as well as emergency rescue squads, etc. To top it all off, after the thing was straightened out, we did not benefit from the event in any way whatsoever. It seems the whole episode coincided with the opening of the motion picture remake of "KING KONG" and the media said it was just a publicity stunt to advertise the movie.

Toward the end of World War II, my grandfather went to work as a supervisor at the old San Antonio Arsenal. This was the primary shopping depot for munitions and armaments that were intended to be sent overseas. We had moved from the southside of San Antonio and things were going well. One day a negligent driver of a fork lift ran over my granddad's right foot both crushing and mangling it. It took the better part of two years to recover and that was something much less than desirable. In fact "Pappy" never really regained the full use of that foot. Having been left crippled he and my Grandmother had to be moved into one of our apartments where they lived until my Grandmother died. Then my Granddad moved in with us. My Grandmother was a raving lunatic at the time of her demise. Although her sight was not impaired, she did not recognize any members of her family. To this very day I still believe that my Grandmother's fanatic enchantment with religion was what drove her over the edge.

I really think that the majority of people in the "nut hut" are there because of our religions. I am not talking about those poor unfortunate individuals with some sort of organic or physiological brain dysfunction. I refer to the common garden variety of psychosis. It seems to me that these folks either wanted to sin so badly, but, for whatever reason, would not allow themselves to do so it drove them insane, or in the alternative, they did sin and felt so guilty about it that it drove them off into outer space.

As active as my grandfather had always been the infirmity

imposed upon him by his bad foot took a terrible toll on him. In addition he felt guilty because he thought that he should be doing more than he could. It was a terribly sad thing to watch a man of his abilities sort of wither away.

Chapter 43

DUANE NELSON AND "THE BYRD"

Duane Nelson is president of Nelson Communications, a Richmond, Virginia-based organization. Duane also has and manages the Byrd Theatre in the 2900 block of Cary Street in Richmond. Now this theatre is listed, historically, as one of the ten most beautiful theatres in America. Duane has created a real miracle with that old theatre. He has restored it to its once glorious self. He has created a clientele that is very similar to those of the '40's and '50's. Patrons receive the "white glove" treatment. Ushers dress and act like those of old. There is no food or drink allowed in the auditorium. Patrons are not allowed to disrupt the performances or movies. They learn from visiting this theatre just what theatrical obedience is all about. They learn when to laugh, applaud, respond, and most importantly, when to be quiet. Customers still line up for blocks to gain admission to the theatre. The wonderful old Wurlitzer theatre organ is still played, after rising from the orchestra pit, between shows. The live shows that appear there are of the very highest quality and it is an experience that everyone should be exposed to at least once just to allow them the right of comparison. Being able to see how life and entertainment was in the past as opposed to how it is today can be very enlightening. I take my hat off to Duane Nelson and wish to heaven that there were more like him.

During the same period of time in which John Daniel was visiting in San Antonio, we decided to go over to Houston, Texas, to the magic convention. Harry Willard wanted to go along. This was only decided a day or two before. Louis Berkie, John Daniel, Torch Towner, Willard, and I went. No one knew we were coming. When we arrived at the auditorium there was a huge crowd. A really extraordinary thing happened. Somehow the word spread through that giant crowd that "Willard was there." As we walked in, the entire audience rose to their feet and gave a standing ovation that must have lasted for 10 minutes. We were all flabbergasted; even I, who knew that Harry Willard's exploits had no boundaries, did not expect that so many others knew.

I remember Willard told me that "as long as people have imaginations there will always be magic, in some form, some of it will be new, some better and a hell of alot of it will be worse!"

During the depression Harry started having all the trucks painted blue. Some had pictorial displays of things like the "Floating Lady" on the side which looked something like a mural but the backgrounds were always blue. I think he said that was because of the times. "Everyone was blue, worried, scared, broke, hungry, depressed" and those blue colors were to let people know that he knew and understood what they were going through. He was well aware of everyone's plight and, for a little while, with magic and humor, he could take them out of it.

A "horse wire" is a betting parlor. These establishments had electronic hookups with the network supplying information of the winner, instantly, at each race track across the nation.

One of the most extensive operations that I ever heard of was my father's horse wire on Snake Hill. This was really a betting room with what looked like bank teller cages. People could simply walk up to one of the cashier's, make a bet on a horse, obtain a receipt and number, then sit back and wait for the outcome of that particular race. They would announce the "winner" over a loudspeaker so everyone could hear. This was not just in the local races at "Alamo Downs" in San Antonio. By special telephone hook up they had direct communications with all of the other racetracks across the country. This would enable a person to place bets on out-of-state horse races. The "room" was just a few doors south of the point where Grayson

Street and North New Braunfels Street intersect. This was the very top of the hill, and I guess, it was named Snake Hill because so many low-life people hung out there. This was incidental to, but not without plan, purpose, and design; the fact that this spot was also the entrance to Fort Sam Houston, one of the oldest and largest military installations in America. This is the garrison where the famous Indian Chief Geronimo was held captive. When the soldiers were paid they almost had to leave by this exit and were exposed to the lures of female pulchitrude, alcoholic spirits, and the availability of most any kind of gambling.

The Snake Hill Bar was next door to the horse wire room. Many would place their bets and retire to the bar to drink while they were awaiting the outcome of a race. Some would imbibe to the point that they forgot about the wager. My father had a fellow working for him known as "Brownie." I never knew him by any other name. Brownie ran errands, took the money back and forth to the "tellers," purchased supplies, made trips to the banks for conversion of smaller bills to larger, etc. Brownie always carried a gun. Brownie was usually withdrawn and did not talk much about what he did for a living but when it came to the gun he was proud to display it and a special holster allowed him to carry it behind his neck. He could casually put both hands up and in a continuum carry through with the motion that produced the weapon in his right hand without anyone standing in front of him, being able to detect where the gun came from. In a straightforward manner he would brag about this special creation of his that was intended as a safety precaution, but, I think, got him killed. Brownie could demonstrate his prowess with the gun and was really fast but apparently, one day, on a trip to the bank he never finished the errand. They found him, minus the two bags of money that he was supposed to be carrying, in an alley with his gun still holstered. Either the perpetrator(s) knew of the existence of the gun or there happened to be more than one assassin.

My father operated his betting room long after the law mandated the closing of "Alamo Downs" race track in San Antonio. He continued taking bets on horse races in all parts of the country. He was a genuine gambler at heart. If there were two birds sitting on a fence he would be willing to bet which one would fly first.

It must have been very hard on him in his declining years to see his hands drawn up into knarly monstrous appendages. The very severe arthritis which overtook him literally forced him to remain rather secluded at the home he adored which was located up in the Salinas Mountains at the "Arroyo Seco" about 50 miles west of Greenfield, California.

All of my father's suits had built in "holdouts." A holdout is a secret pocket or device to hold hidden dice or cards. One was generally behind his lapels. Often there was, at least, one at a seam in either the shoulder or trouser leg. He had the arm "gimmicks" also. There are contrivances which strap to the arm and a connection either running down the pantleg to the foot or to the opposite hand. By moving the leg, or the arm, this "machine" can extend, or withdraw, in a "lazy Susan" fashion, a rod that has an attachment at the end which could grab a card (or cards) and pull them up the sleeve or, alternatively, deliver cards to the hand. These marvels were usually constructed by someone who manufactured surgical instruments and were very expensive.

There was a retired colonel living in Florida who had a reputation as a poker player. He could NEVER lose. Several gamblers from San Antonio decided that they wanted to see this man in action. They called and were ecstatic when given an invitation to come for a game. They were all given mint juleps by the colonel's man servant. The man, who seemed to perform the function of a butler, kept everyone well "oiled" with alcohol. What the Colonel did seemed to transcend all logic and dexterity. He just never seemed to lose. One of the players excused himself and very quietly followed the man servant out to the enormous kitchen were the drinks were mixed. While spying on the butler he saw the man "stacking" a deck of cards to allow for the dealing of winning hands. Then the cards were inserted into a secret compartment in the tray where the drinks were carried. The tray would, for but an instant, be set upon the deck on the table. In that short period one deck was exchanged for the other. When this was discovered the fellow that did the "spying" went out to the car and got a bottle of glue. He came back and went directly to the kitchen. This was a huge, old souther mansion so they could not be overheard. He grabbed the butler and told him that if he did not do exactly as he was told that he intended to kill him on the spot. The butler agreed. They glued all the cards together, each one glued to the top of another, and then the deck was slipped into the secret part of the tray. The butler was instructed to continue as usual. The man that did the threatening went back and took his seat at the table. The butler did the "switch" and when the Colonel picked up the deck and tried to deal a hand of cards the top card simply would not come off the deck. The "spy" pulled out a revolver and laid it on the table saying "Colonel, I have heard of a lot of "cold" decks (a term applied to trick decks or stacked decks) but I have never heard of one that was frozen solid." Everyone laughed, except the Colonel. The San Antonio delegation left with their money.

Chapter 44

A BANNER MAN

Show card writers seem to have, pretty much, vanished from the current scene. These were people who had the unique ability to sit down and take a piece of poster board and simply write the most beautiful, elaborate small posters... ever. These cards were frequently seen in various departments of large stores as well as wherever specialized signs were needed. They could do this lettering (or writing) without guide lines or layout.

Banner men were something else. These people could do the same thing as a show card writer except they did it on a very large scale. They would paint the huge advertising banners often seen in and about rodeos, circuses, race car tracks, etc. They could also letter the side of a semi-truck with just a step ladder, paint, and brushes. These signs looked as though they had been very carefully blocked off and laid out. Not so. They would simply get up on that ladder and write those gigantic letters. Something that always amazed me. Harry Willard had such a man in Hixon. I never knew his first name. He paid his own way by going in ahead of the show and selling large advertising space to merchants to be displayed in and around the show. He would leave the show's part of the money and the completed signs with the sponsor in each town to be erected the day of the show.

Willard used to say, "Give Hixon a bottle of wine and he could re-paint the Cistine Chapel and probably do a better job." I really doubt that, but who knows?

Harry told me that these banner writers did not see the world the same as others. He said that a banner man could see the whole picture from the outset and it was very precise. One time he actually went around and measured the space between letters on one of Hixon's big billboards. The spaces and letters were exact, yet it had been done without any kind of guideline or anything else. They simply painted it as they saw it in their head. Incredible!

Chapter 45

WHEN I WAS ALEXANDER

Before I became Brandon, I used the name "Alexander the Great." Not "The Great Alexander the Man Who Knows;" I did not even know another Alexander had ever existed outside of general history. When it was pointed out to me by the great Howard Campbell (Howard's Fun Shop of Houston, Texas) during an engagement, I stopped using the title immediately following the Houston engagement. Howard Campbell was a really terrific fellow and a wonderful magician for children. He made a lot of money which did him absolutely no good at all because he always managed to lose all of it betting on horse races. Some of my very best memories are of Howard Campbell.

While playing the Uptown Theatre in Houston under the name of "Alexander the Great," I became acquainted with a young black fellow who worked for the theatre as custodian and ran errands for Mr. Fred Cannata, the owner. I do not recall this young man's name but he either could not, or would not, remember my stage name and continually called me "Alludah the Great." We generally used a lot of flashpots. Audiences like to see flashes of fire and smoke go off and something magical happen. For some weird reason the black kid never managed to see the whole show even though we were doing four shows a day. During the flash parts he always seem to be missing or off doing something else. Finally the last day of the three-day engagement he was clowning around backstage, calling me "Alludah," and accidently tripped the release on the flash pots never realizing what he had done. The flashes and puffs went off, he screamed, composed himself, and apologized with a promise to never call me "Alludah" again.

Chapter 46

A SUBMARINE INVASION OF SAN ANTONIO

In high school, brother Alfred Schnepp taught physics and chemistry. A brilliant man, Schnepp, had contributed to the Manhattan Project and ran his classes with an iron hand. He treated his students like they were in the military and he, quite literally, made sure everyone really "got it." He would tolerate no failures. We learned and we learned good. Some of us were not too happy with the strict authoritarian and disciplinarism on Schnepp's part. Still, looking back on it, I am convinced that unless the teacher wants to produce "numbskulls," there are some who must be treated as Schnepp treated us and there is simply no other way regardless of what the powers that be allege.

Well, toward the end of the course, a couple of us decided to try and get back at Schnepp, sort of. One afternoon we went into the lab after school and stole a large chunk of metallic Sodium (atomic weight 11)... at least I think it was Sodium. Schnepp kept it in a gigantic glass jar under oil, or kerosene, or some such. During lecture he would use a pen knife to take, ever so small, a tiny sliver of this stuff and drop it into some water. The element looked like a lump of rust but underneath its coating it was bright, shiny metal. When this smallest amount imaginable touched the water, it went crazy. It would run around on the surface of the water popping, exploding, making waves, and doing all kinds of really crazy stuff. A buddy, who shall remain nameless because he eventually became a highly successful and respected attorney, went with me down to the San Antonio River. That river winds through the center of downtown San Antonio and tourists can take gondola rides up and down the river to see the city by boat. It is a charming excursion which I heartily recommend to anyone. Well, to get on with my story, my comrade, with whom I had grown up, and I went out to the middle of the bridge on Houston Street (the main artery of the city) made sure no one was looking, and we dropped all of that stuff into the San Antonio River. Boy you never saw anything like it. That glob of metal went racing up and down the river, hitting embankments and bouncing off, exploding, screaming, smoking, churning up waves and it created a panic. Someone called the fire department, police, emergency ambulance services, etc. By now the bridge was jammed full of people. We were up on a fire escape on the side of the old Texas Theatre, laughing like hell, watching these proceedings. We came down, sauntered out on the bridge, and heard one of the Mexican firemen tell another that he thought it was some kind of miniature Nazi submarine going up the river to try to blow up the city. Any fool would have known better because the river was only about 8 to 10 feet deep; but, that nonsense circulated through the crowd and set off a second panic. Everyone cleared the bridge in a hurry--everyone except us. Several others from our school were standing nearby and when my associate in crime, and I, did not run that must have been what tipped them off that we were the culprits. I have suspicions, of course, but could not prove who "finked" on us; but, the very next day Schnepp was waiting for us when we got to school. We each drew a three-day suspension and the loss of some of our privileges. We also had to reimburse the school for the element which, as I recall, was expensive. Still I think that it was worth it.

My son, Don, Jr., is a handsome lad with a scholarly bent and appearance. He never exhibited any inclination toward magic or any of its subdivisions. I never urged him to do so. He has his psychology degrees and has made a highly significant place for himself in the computer world having developed a method by which a 360 mainframe can double its maximum output. This has been a God send for the larger companies contemplating the purchase of an additional 360. He and his family of three children and wife Susan, live in Lexington, Massachusetts. They own rental property in Melrose, Massachusetts. It was during one of our visits to Boston that we went out to see the marvelous "Le Grand David and His Own Spectacular Magic Show" in Beverly, Massachusetts. This bedroom city of Boston, was a lot like most American towns today. The downtown area exhibited large numbers of closed and boarded up businesses, which had been thriving only a few years earlier. The "Le Grand David" show changed a lot of that. By providing the public with an inordinate number of large illusions and a huge cast, this show has acquired a world-wide reputation. Now visitors come from all over the world to see the show. The main reason for the success of that show is the fact that the performance is included in all bus tours of New England. They have managed to include the assistance of the Department of Tourism and, thusly, have developed this magic show into a genuine tourist attraction. Kilpatrick, a young man on the staff of the show, is largely responsible for this very interesting piece of work.

Chapter 47

NOT ALICE'S GEORGE...
A DIFFERENT GOEBEL

One of the all time great stage illusionists lives in Baltimore, Maryland. I do not mean glitz, flashing lights, and loud racket (excuse me, music) but real, honest, stellar, all-time GREAT illusionists. His name is George Goebel. *(See Appendix A-18)* There is not the slightest doubt that George could easily have been placed in the upper ranks alongside Dante, Blackstone, Sr., Willard, and the others. George demonstrated the intelligence NOT to accept road tours and stay at home with his family and operate one of the most successful costume businesses in the nation. Jones Costumes furnishes costuming for the fine opera companies and he does it very, very well. I envy him and his foresight.

One of George Goebel's closest friends is a fellow named Mark Walker. Mark is probably the most dedicated magical historian around. Mark does not have any official title in connection with his collection and preserving of the memorabilia arising out of magic but that has nothing to do with his love of it and great diligence in his pursuits. I salute him and his work.

Chapter 48

BE CAREFUL FLOSSING . . .
AND I DO NOT MEAN YOUR TEETH

I think almost everyone is familiar with floss candy. Sometimes they call it cotton candy. It is fine strands of sugar. These strands become big piles of what appears to be colored cotton and it is wrapped around a paper cone. It is delicious. Ordinary granulated table sugar is colored with food coloring. A small amount of the colored sugar is placed in a round cup-like metal container with lots of tiny holes in the sides of it. A heating unit beneath the metal cup of sugar heats it until it is a liquid and then it is spun at high speed so that the centrifugal force slings the liquid (melted) sugar out through the little holes. As soon as the hot liquid sugar hits the cooler air, it again solidifies creating the strands of colored sugar. A large pan (about two feet in diameter) accumulates the strands as they are slung around where the vendor grabs handfuls of the "cotton candy" and wraps it around the paper cone. Then it is placed up for sale. One or two people usually handle such an undertaking; however, on the really big circus this candy must be produced in very high volume and speed. They have machines many times larger and faster than those normally seen in shopping malls, special events, carnivals, small circus, etc. Some of these larger machines operate on 220 voltage and require several people to grab the candy and toss it onto the cones. There is no speed control and it must be done very quickly. I DID NOT know any of this when it was suggested, by one of our sponsors, that as a special treat for all of the youngsters attending our show, they would receive a free cone of cotton candy. Boy, what a nightmare that was!

The only person in that particular area of Texas with a floss candy machine was in the hospital. He had been off the road during the winter season. He could not bring his cotton candy machine to the auditorium and make the candy but he did agree to let the sponsor themselves rent his machine and make the candy. The man had his wife bring his truck over about 12 noon the day of the show. Sponsoring members unloaded it and set it up in the lobby of the auditorium. The wife sort of explained how it operated. The one thing that she failed to impress on the sponsors was the speed of the machine and the need for many more than one person to operate it.

They got it all ready to go, put the sugar in, and started it up just as the first patrons started to arrive. Then all hell broke loose. That stuff started bubbling up over the sides and down onto the floor. The weather was too cold for air conditioning but the circulating fans were running. Those fans picked up the little wisps of candy which were floating in the air by now and circulated them around pretty good. The floors became sticky with candy. Everyone's hair did likewise as well as the walls, seats... everything. Thank heaven the front curtain of the stage was closed, otherwise, the sticky stuff would have covered our scenery, costumes, equipment, and of course, us. I heard screams from the lobby so I ran up there. Mountains of candy were all over. I grabbed a pressure water hose off the wall and turned it on. It was not a fire hose but much more powerful than the average garden hose. I started to wet down the candy which melted immediately upon contact with the water... the people I hit with the water did not melt too well. Everyone was soaking wet and still sticky. Most people were madder 'n hell. It cost an extra $200 to have the cleanup crew come and clean everything between shows. Betcha they never did get it all off.

Chapter 49

RAMON AND CHENCHO

Raymond Mendez is a wonderful young magician. *(See Appendix A-19)* He makes a nice appearance and conducts himself well on stage. Under the guidance of my dear old friend, John Taacha (pronounced TAH-HAH), who owns the Bureau of Lectures and Concert Artists, Raymond made long cross country tours.

Raymond Mendez travelled with our show for two seasons as stage manager and assistant. He and a magic clown called Chencho had a well-known act in the south.

During the periods in which Ray Mendez travelled with us, we had another young man named Rudy Torres. Rudy was an exact double for the well-known singer, Tony Orlando. Every place he went girls followed him and asked for his autograph. He was shy so this embarrassed him to no end. Scores of young girls came to our show just to see Rudy. He finally quit because he could not stand the pestering any longer; but, the last I heard, Rudy was trying to learn to sing... you guessed it... like Tony Orlando.

Chapter 50

ABOUT MEL-ROY

There was a man named Holly. His initials were W.W., but no one ever seemed to know what they stood for. In fact, I am not sure that his name was really Holly. I do not think that anyone else knows that for positive. Anyway Holly adopted the name Mel-Roy. That was something of a stage name. He had been on radio stations all around the country prognosticating and claiming to be a mind reader. He would claim to tell listener's fortunes over the air waves. He finally lit in Del Rio, Texas. At that time in the late '20's, there was a radio transmitter that was so powerful that it is said to have reached the entire North American continent. I think that the call letters of the station in Del Rio were KEX. Mel-Roy went to the station owner and sold him on the idea of doing occult mind reading bits on the station. He would answer the questions of his listeners over the air, if they mailed the query in with a fee. I think it was a dollar. I have seen a photograph of a long table with about 15 to 20 ladies sitting around it, each with a bushel basket on either side. They would open the envelopes, put the question in one basket and the money in the other. The United States Postal authorities actually had to put on an additional four mail trucks just to take the letters over to that radio station each day. It is said that Mel-Roy was actually receiving more than 15,000 letters each weekday. I do not think they could have arrested him had he simply told his listeners they would receive a reply by mail if he happened to be unable to answer them on the air. Printed stock form replies would have probably sufficed. Anyway, authorities put an end to his mind reading exploits.

Mel-Roy was not content with the millions of dollars he took in with his radio mind reading. He had seen the Willard show and was very envious. He wanted to be able to do what Willard did. He tried to hire Willard to teach him, but he refused. Mel-Roy called Floyd Thayer, in Los Angeles, and told him that if he would not take any other orders for magic equipment until he had filled the Mel-Roy requests, that Mel-Roy would pay him to build one of everything in the Thayer catalog. That agreement was said to have been reached. That equipment was shipped to Mel-Roy at Del Rio, the world's largest jig-saw puzzle. Mel-Roy could not figure out how to assemble most of the illusions. He called Harry and offered him a very large sum of money just to come down and set up the tricks for him. Harry went and spent the greater part of a week erecting the equipment. He hung around long enough watching Mel-Roy rehearse to know that it simply was not going to work. Harry went back to San Antonio.

Mel-Roy had semi-trucks with specially built trailers to carry his show. He did not think things through. He had the trailers constructed 44' long. That was longer than the law would allow. He had to obtain special permission just to try and move his equipment from Del Rio over to Uvalde. The roads in those days were not landscaped to handle such long vehicles. When one of those trailers would come to a railroad track, the cab and front wheels would pass over the track alright, but the rear wheels could not make it. The trailer would be stuck on the railroad track like a see-saw. After the first episode they had to unload everything and have moving and storage companies come and continue the drayage to Uvalde.

A friend of Willard's who was living in Uvalde, reported to him on the show. Harry said that after the first performance the number attending each show was less than 50. That Mel-Roy did well on the radio where he could not be seen but in person it was another thing altogether. The man was just plain "clunky." He did not have the demeanor, voice, bearing, stage presence, attitude, or anything else necessary for such an undertaking. He found it to be true in short order. Mel-Roy did succeed in hiring a number of fairly capable

175

magicians to lay out his string of dates. Even Tommy Willard did the show for Mel-Roy for a while.

The thing seems to have come to an abrupt halt when Mel-Roy undertook appearances at the State Fair of Texas. There were to be outdoor stage shows in the terrible heat of Dallas. What Mel-Roy planned to do was to load the female assistants into the trick compartments of the illusions such as the doll house, glass casket, sawing a woman base, etc. Then stage hands were to lift these contraptions up onto the stage. The trick was to be performed and then lifted down again. These women would pass out and one almost died in a hospital. Mel-Roy would open a trick cabinet and the female assistant would come tumbling out onto the stage in a dead faint. The other shows had to be cancelled. This is a pretty good illustration of Mel-Roy's thinking and the problems that follow from not giving such a situation proper consideration. Either he could not, or he would not, think things through. Still he accomplished something with his radio mind reading that has never been duplicated or equaled.

Chapter 51

IN DEFENSE OF FONES

Frank Sterling (The Great Mahendra) introduced me to George Pughe. Pughe was a good-sized man with a dapper moustache that looked much like the one worn by George Marquis. Pughe was a magical enthusiast and a magician of sorts, but will be best remembered for having been the creator of telephone solicitation promotions as they applied to showbusiness. From all that I have been able to learn, historically, George Pughe was the man that commenced the sale of tickets and advertising to shows, exhibits, attractions, events, and whatever. His first such promotion was with the old dance marathons which he called, appropriately, "Dance-athons." These were things in which a sponsor, such as the American Legion, would advertise for couples to dance as long as they could. The couple left standing would win a prize which was generally $100-$200 for this grueling experience. I know that the prize does not seem like very much today, but back in the '20's it was like several thousand dollars would be in 1995. Sometimes these poor people would dance for days. They would, quite literally, be holding each other up. When it was over, some actually had to go to the hospital. Pughe would have his people get on the telephone and call every merchant and individual, that had a telephone, and ask them to help out the sponsor and buy some tickets or advertising for the affair. He was so successful that the method quickly spread to all forms of showbusiness including, but not limited to air shows, ice shows, legitimate roadshows, magic shows, circuses, etc. Fortunes were made using this tool. The success of the well-known Shrine Circus was accomplished by using telephone promotions.

Almost from the beginning the phone promo was brought under great criticism. I think it was mostly from some money-grubbing merchants that simply did not want to part with philan-thropic money but did not want the public to know how "greedy" and "tight" they were. They started to circulate the rumor that in these promotions some criminal-minded promoters were hauling tons of money out of town and the poor sponsor was not being paid anything for his trouble. This fabrication was magnified and some citizen's watchdog groups came into existence to police such things. Investigation usually proved the so-called watchdog bureau to be a small group of businessmen either trying to control the solicitation or put it out of business. These very people later started to lay claim to their being advocates of consumers. There was never a single case, in this nation, wherein a proper investigation revealed them taking any kind of action against one of their members for failing to stand behind his goods or services. They were really created to protect each other in whatever scam or fraud they happened to be perpetrating on the public. It is also noted that their attacks, and the degree thereof, were directly related to the power of the sponsoring organization. You rarely heard of them attacking a police association for selling the ads and tickets to their "Policemen's Ball;" but' the poor little podunk Blind People's Association came under repeated attack for calling people on the telephone to ask for money.

Today we can scarcely find a day wherein we do not receive at least one telephone call soliciting us for something all the way from credit cards to light bulbs. It has become a much abused method of doing business and a multi-billion dollar a year operation.

Still I doubt that most people will, of their own free will, go out of their way to buy a light bulb to help the blind, buy a ticket to see one of the smaller circuses, buy a broom from the Boys Club, etc. They just will not do it unless, or until, they are "put on the spot," so to speak, and personally asked to help out or contribute. In the first place they do not really know, for sure, who is on the other end of the line. For all they know it could be their banker's wife, a patrolman from their own neighborhood, a kid from "up the street," or someone to whom they have applied for a loan. This causes them to at least seriously consider the proposition.

Antagonists of the phone deal lead the public to believe that these "rich, criminal promoters" who are cleaning out the city's coffers take the money away with them by the truckload. NOT TRUE! Let me break it down for you so that you can see where the money really goes and why it is so easy for these detractors to scare people and try to convince them not to participate in the campaign.

The average telephone room must have about ten telephones for each 100,000 population. This also depends on how long the sponsor intends to conduct the campaign. Six weeks to three months is about average. Some operate continually all year long. For the sake of this discussion, let us say that the town has about one million in habitants and it is a six-week campaign. They will have two large office spaces with a smaller business office between the two. They will install the appropriate number of telephones, rent office furniture and equipment, have index cards written on every number in the telephone directory, have printing (envelopes, stationary, invoices, letters of explanation, tickets, etc.) prepared, purchase vast quantities of postage, arrange for the rental of the auditorium, run advertise-ments for help, and all of the other necessary things that must be done in order to conduct a successful campaign. The largest expense by far, is the employees. That is especially true of those that actually do the telephoning. These people are referred to as "phonemen" although there are as many females as there are males. These are young people of about the same calibre as those employed by the fast food chains. Such youngsters are generally paid between $5 and $7 an hour. At $5 an hour a room with 20 telephones costs $100 for each hour that it operates. Simply stated, for two 8-hour crews the daily salaries for the "phonemen" would run about $1,600 per day. I am sure that you can see an expense of $45,000 to $60,000 run up right away. That is before the promotor or sponsor makes a nickel. In each sales "pitch" the goal, purposes, ethic, and all pertinent information concerning the sponsor is given to each prospective customer. It is not just a sales job. It is a public relations campaign explaining what it is all about. The Supreme Court of the United States has ruled that such undertaking frequently costs as much as 95% of the gross just to raise the money. The prime thrust gives employment to young people who would otherwise not be able to have such work. It also teaches them a trade. All this is in addition to the money being raised for the sponsoring organization.

The truth of the matter is that the telemarket organizations do a terrific job not just raising funds for those who cannot, or will not, do it themselves, but of creating public awareness that could not otherwise be purchased at any price.

There are, to be sure, unscrupulous individuals in tele-marketing just as there are in every other business. For the most part, the telephone promotors are honest, hard working, and deserving of support.

Let me tell you about one who was NOT deserving. A couple of promoters in New York started calling people on the telephone and telling the potential customer that they had located the wife of the UNKNOWN SOLDIER AND THE POOR WOMAN WAS ABSOLUTELY DESTITUTE AND HOMELESS. They were trying to raise enough money to make a down payment on a home for her, and perhaps, even an outright purchase. They were taking in money in very large amounts. Finally the police found out about it and stopped them with a long jail sentence. I could never understand anyone believing that there was a wife of the unknown soldier. There were thousands of unknown soldiers. That is simply a term applied to all those men killed in action who were buried in unmarked graves. This kind of travesty deserves the very greatest sanctions imposed upon it that society can produce.

Chapter 52

MEMORIES

Ah yes, memories, I must have enough to fill several other books. I remember John Bradshaw... "Old Doc Bradshaw" and his "Olde Tyme Medicine Show"... John has sold his particular brand of "hocum" all the way from Coney Island to the Philippine Islands. He is a magician, juggler, fire eater, comic, pitchman, musician (a guitarist of real note), and snake oil peddlar--that is with a real snake. He loved the startled looks on people's faces, friends, and foes alike, when they came up to his truck and were suddenly greeted, face to face, with his pet lion. It broke his heart when he was forced to get rid of the animal. John can tell some of the most outrageous stories in the world.

I remember Todd Vess ("jack of all trades and master to none"). He was the best stage manager I ever had until he became so enamored of himself that he lost all reason. He completely forgot the main thrust of whatever endeavor he found himself involved with at the moment. He would actually forget about the show because he would be so caught up with some little nonsensical thing. He would let the show die in order to play with whatever pet project caught his fancy at the moment. Still a very great talent and so knowledgeable that I would doubt that there is very much about show business that he does not know.

I remember a very strange Thanksgiving at the Chatham Hotel in Kansas City. When I say strange I mean Strange... Glenn Strange, Frankenstein's Monster. Glenn grew up on a ranch in Clyde, Texas, and his main (and favorite) fare was Mexican food. Back in 1951 there were not many Mexican restaurants outside of Texas. When I lived in Hollywood, I had to drive over an hour to the only such cafe that I ever found in Los Angeles County. Anyway, on the Thanksgiving in question, Glenn and I agreed that traditional turkey was not appealing. So we went out and bought all of the ingredients and started cooking a giant Mexican dinner. The smell of that food wafted through the upper corridors and elevator shaft of the entire hotel. This is a very refined, sedate establishment. Apparently, the tenants had little or no exposure to quality Mexican grub. They started stopping by the door of our suite asking what it was and could they please sample it. We gave away so much that we scarcely had any left for ourselves. We both agreed that second to showbusiness Mexican food was probably the way to go. Today it has become so popular, nationwide, that I would doubt that there is a hamlet of any size, in America, without a "Taco Bell" or some such establishment. And no, "Taco Bell" is not the Mexican telephone company.

I remember taking a wrong turn in the middle of the night and getting off on a very narrow road that would not allow for us turning our truck around or backing down. We were forced to go on up and up... almost right up until we reached the summit, with a near burned-up motor in one vehicle, on top of a mountain in a genuine "ghost town" named Jerome, Arizona.

I remember standing in the backyard under our pecan trees putting a new coat of paint on a "Girl without a Middle" illusion and listening to the radio. Suddenly, the voice of President Franklin Roosevelt broke into the program and explained that following the "dastardly sneak attack on Pearl Harbor by the Japanese had left America with no alternative than to declare that a 'state of war' now existed between Japan and the United States."

I remember holding my little newborn son in my arms for the first time--and experiencing a feeling that I have never had before nor since.

I remember the "Secret of the Big Indian." I think that I have told you about when my Aunt Ollie and her mother, my Great Aunt

Pinky, lived by the Willard family. After Aunt Pinky died, Aunt Ollie moved to Highland Park. Wherever she lived, all my life, she had this really big American Indian statue in her living room. Usually it was next to her grandfather clock. I never liked the grandfather clock; I thought it was dumb. Besides, it always woke me while I was trying to sleep. The Indian, well, that was something else. He was a little taller than a real man. His skin was almost bronze. He was dressed only in a headdress like Indian Chiefs wore and a loin cloth. He was barefooted. You are not going to believe what I am going to tell you. No matter where you walked in the room that Indian's eyes followed you. I know it sounds crazy but they really did. It was not until I was grown and Aunt Ollie had moved to Highland Park, that I found out what was causing it. Learning the secret of the Indian helped me create what became our most effective theatre lobby display. When the day came that I was able to get right up in the statue's face and peer into his eyes, I saw what was happening. The eyeballs were concave and not convex, like humans It was that simple.

Now let me tell you how we sort of shocked tens of thousands of people with the spook mummy. I went to our local department store, Joskee's of Texas. It was the largest and the finest in town. The window dresser there was a relative of mine and he got me a full-sized male replica used in store window displays. During that period they were very popular and most big stores had warehouses full of them. I took the mannequin and removed its head. I very carefully etched out the eyes with an electric drill. Then I went to the local novelty store and bought a glass eye. Kids would buy these and clamp it over their real eye and hold it there in place by squinting their eye. It looked like that child had his eye popping out of his head. Some of the unfortunate people that had lost an eye would have one of these glass eyes placed in their sightless socket rather than wear a patch over the missing eye. I took the glass eye and made a cast of it by covering it in a fine coating of Vaseline and inserting it into a small container of dental plaster. When the plaster hardened, I took my glass eye and did it all over again. Then I had two negative casts of human eyes. I ground off the plaster that was superfluous and fit each of these concave eye balls behind the eye openings in what would have been the place for the eye socket in a real human being. I glued each piece in place, waited for it to dry and then I took the hollow head and filled it half full of "Plaster of Paris." When that plaster hardened, I took the head to my dear old friend, Forest Noltz, at the General Art and Process Company and had him take one of his very small paint brushes and paint the convacity snow white. It took three or four coats of paint. When the white paint was dry, I had Forest, ever so carefully, paint the iris and the pupil in each "eye." Then the eyelining and decorating made it look, from just a few feet away, like you were really looking at the eyes. I replaced the head on my dummy body. We wrapped the whole thing in bandages similar to the "Ace" bandage used for medicinal purposes. We gave the bandages a light coating of grey spray paint. When that dried we gave it another coating of light brown paint. We would put this thing in a "mummy case" and set it in a darkened corner of the inner theatre lobbies. A small green spotlight illuminated the face and eyes. Passersby got the eerie impression that the eyes of the mummy were following them. I have actually heard people shriek, "That thing keeps looking at me." Very effective, and I have often wondered why no one else ever used it.

Chapter 53

CUTTING UP WOMEN WITH SAWS

"I used to do those tricks where the magician saws a girl in half. I did it with my sister... now she is my half sister." YUK... YUK... YUK. So it goes. One of the oldest, yet most profound, magical illusions is the one in which a magician seemingly saws a lady into two separate halves. There are many versions of the trick; most are more than well known. The most popular box model, known as the "Thin model" is thoroughly exposed and every phase of the presentation of the trick is replicated on video tape in the "Mystery Magician" by Fox Video and, I assume, available in most video stores. The best of the box methods did not hold a great deal of interest for me. If a magician is going to saw someone in half why hide her in a box? Why not just lay her out on a table and do the dirty deed? The instant the audience sees the box, they know something fishy is going on. The exception is the Thurston, Dante, Willard method which was more of a comedy act that a trick. The two portions of the young lady's body are, apparently separated and the upper half of the young lady starts giggling and complaining that the spectator holding her foot is tickling her. This generally happens when one half of her is on one side of the stage and the other half is on the other side.

My favorite is the buzz saw. This is presented by laying the girl on a table, putting a four inch wide board beneath her middle,

185

starting a giant 30 inch buzz saw and shoving the screaming blade through her body. After the "surgery" the magician pulls the board out from beneath the girl and shows the audience that the saw not only passed through her body, but that the saw actually cut the board in half also.

Aldo Richiardi, Jr. had a most impressive method of accomplishing this. Instead of having the girl lay face down, as in most models, he had her on her back. The saw was started and ripped through her middle parts. Blood would fly 20 feet in all directions. He would then stop the performance and invite the audience to come up and walk across the stage and look at the corpse. Assistants put up a rope barrier, but the people wishing to take a closer look could come within a foot or two of the illusion. The saw blade was still resting in the center of the unfortunate female's body with the entrails and blood popping out. People would actually faint at the sight. He added to this possibility by having an assistant, in the wings, heat some ether in a small metal saucer apparatus over a candle. The odor combined with the ghastly sight before them was simply too much for some to bear.

Richiardi accomplished this in a truly unique way. There was no mechanical gimmick. There are people who can do the vanishing stomach act. They are actually able to suck their entire stomach up into the chest cavity--so much so that the back bone can be see from the front. This is how it was done. At the right time the girl sucked in her tummy and a metal band afforded a degree of protection from the spinning blade. A side of trimmed veal or lamb was strapped to the girl's front side with a sack of stage blood and fake entrails. When the blade hit the contents of the real flesh and bone strapped onto the girls front, the audience would swear they were seeing this horrible act take place. I am not sure how much protection the metal would have been--it was sort of thick and the blade was strong. I even heard one the girls say, "If she sneezes, we're sunk!"

I have vacillated between the "Rip Saw Decapitation" and the "Visible Buzz Saw." I have performed both of them. I will explain the sawing in half instead of the decapitation because, although it was not as gruesome, it did look very authentic.

In my buzz saw illusion, a lady would walk out to the center of the stage. This assistant would apparently be hypnotized and the curtain would open revealing the torture device. It was a long table that appeared to be very thin but, in fact, was deep enough at the middle to allow the lady to drop her center down into the table. It looked impossible for this table to be thick enough to conceal anything but it truly did. A metal plate approximately three inches wide and long enough to reach across the table could be slid out of its special groove. It slid out to the back where it could not be seen by the audience. The lady was lifted up and placed, face down, on the table. She had to keep herself rigid while the male assistants lifted her up onto the table, otherwise the audience would see the trick fake back that she had strapped (with wide elastic bands) to her under the costume. Once in place on the table I would slide the metal plate out allowing her to lower her middleparts into the table. The fake back remained at table level and visible to the spectators. The metal plate was then slid back across the table to act as a safety precaution from the whirling blade. A piece of wood about the same size as the metal plate was placed underneath the fake back but appeared as though it was under the subjects real tummy. We would start the motor and run the saw through the lady after raising the upper part of her costume in order to expose the bare (fake) midriff. The spinning saw was pushed, on its own separate rolling frame, across the table and completely through the woman's (fake) back. Then the strip of wood was removed to show the audience that the saw really did pass through her as it had cut the board beneath her in half. The upper half of the costume was then pulled down, the lady lifted off the table and awakened from her trance (?) and she bowed as the curtain closed.

Previously I mentioned the "thin model" box method of the "sawing" which is so popular today. I am pretty sure that this "thin" sawing is attributed to my dear old friend John Daniel. John has one of the most fertile magical minds around. I remember the story that one day he was supposed to have been in Florida (I think) and after having exhausted other avenues found himself in the position of having to present a cremation illusion that very day. By himself John took a skill saw, wood, and other supplies and constructed a super cremation illusion. He was not satisfied with it. He wanted the apparatus to look more gruesome so he went to a novelty store and purchased a bunch of plastic Halloween skulls. He cut a large hold in the top of each skull and one under each chin. Then he slid the skulls, one on top of another, down the pipe legs on the illusion so that when he was finished the illusion appeared to be sitting on these stacks of human skulls... very, very, clever.

I am pretty sure that at least one version of a "sawing" arose out of John Daniel seeing an illusion in Europe (Germany, I think) which he told me about. John said that the magician had his assistants place a very thick sheet of clear glass on two supports. Then a lady came out and would lie down on the glass and allow herself to be covered, from neck to ankles, with sand. The magician would then scoop out the sand and the audience was aghast over the fact that her middle part was gone. At the time we discussed it we, sort of, decided that it had to be like Richiardi's buzz saw and the lady really could do the vanishing tummy act.

Chapter 54

MY GOODNESS, HOW SMART OUR PARENTS BECOME AS WE GROW OLDER!

As a child, I remember thinking why did the older folks in my family have the right to tell me how I was supposed to do anything. They had screwed up their lives so, obviously, they were not so smart. I found it hard to believe just how smart they became as I grew older-- probably bordered on brilliance. Thinking back over some of the things they told me, I now find them to be deeply rooted in fact and logic.

When I was very young--I think in the first grade--I noticed that a lot of children came barefoot during the warm weather. One little boy, I believe his name was Johnny Green, always wore just a piece of leather that had holes punched all around the top edge and a stout string running through them. When the strings were pulled tight and tied, they remained on the child's feet like a shoe or something that might be worn by native American Indians. One day I asked him why he did not wear regular shoes. He said, "'cause my daddy does not have money to buy me any." At recess I sat down on a playground curb and took off my shoes and insisted that the boy wear them. I went barefoot the rest of the day. When I reached home after school, my grandmother had a fit wanting to know where my shoes were. When I explained what had happened, she took a switch and whipped me until it drew blood. That very night the boys father came to the door and returned the shoes. My grandmother tried to be nice and told him that I had another pair and it was alright for his son to keep them. He said, "No ma'am... we will not accept handouts... we will just make do with what we have until things get better..." MAKE DO WITH WHAT WE HAVE... that seems to be a group of words that have been lost today.

My Grandmother was mean as hell. I remember one time after we had moved out to a bedroom city called "South San" that she wanted some bacon. She ordered my Grandfather to go and buy some. It was bitterly cold so he put on his overcoat, hat, gloves, and scarf and went out and tried to start the car. In those days it was sometimes impossible to start old cars until the weather warmed up. Lots of people drained their radiators every night in order to keep them from freezing. Granddad's car would not start. That man had to walk in that terrible weather and buy her some bacon. It was a long way. When he returned and gave her the bacon she screamed, "You old fool... this stuff still has the rind on it... it is not even sliced... you take it back and exchange it right now!" My Grandfather just sat down on the edge of his bed and cried big tears which I watched run down his cheeks. I put on my coat, mittens, cap, etc. and told him that I would walk with him. He would not let me go, I think mainly because of my poor health. He made that ferocious trip again and exchanged the bacon. I have not, to this day, been able to overcome my feelings of just, how on earth, my Grandmother could be so mean.

I went through a long period during which I sort of held it against my mother for having married, and remarried, so many times. As the years have passed I have come to understand that, more than anything else, she could not stand loneliness and was merely trying to avoid it.

Chapter 55

PROBLEMS WITH TRAVELING ACTORS

We were always having problems with girls on the show. This was especially true where we played several days in one town. Some local fellow would take one of the girls out and the next thing we knew she was leaving the show to get married, or she was pregnant, or whatever. A girl answered an ad in New Mexico and traveled with us for several weeks until one day the Sheriff was waiting for us. How anyone found out that she was with us I do not know unless she had told them. She was arrested for child abandonment and later for attempted murder. She had been living out on a farm which was located a long distance from any town or neighbors when her husband left one morning and never returned. After a couple of days she was frantic. She did not even have a telephone. The family was running out of food and she just started walking. The mental strain must have been too much for her because she just kept walking until she arrived at the stage door of the show asking for a job... any job... I gave one to her. I did not know that she had left three tiny children behind alone in that old house. Accidently a couple of days later the postman found the children and called the authorities. Very strange.

We had a girl named JoAnn. She bunked with two other girls

on the show. All swore to me that JoAnn never dated anyone either on the show or along the way. Nevertheless, about four and a half months out on the tour that year she started "showing" and she confided to my wife that she was, in fact, pregnant--which by that time was perfectly obvious. She gave us no notice and simply said she was leaving to get married in Oregon. She did and later wrote to us telling us that she had gotten pregnant the day before she left to go on the road with us. The next season we attempted to avoid the hassle by taking an entirely different tact. We only hired people of the gay persuasion. They were difficult to recruit in those days. Once we hired on a crew and broke them in they worked out perfectly. There did seem to be a reversal of roles backstage because a person would see young men ironing costumes, sewing, pressing, folding, loading trick flowers, decorating equipment, etc... things normally associated with the female gender and then there would be girls up on ladders, in catwalks, handling crates, setting up heavy illusions, using hammers, saws, all kinds of tools, etc... doing those things which one might associate with the masculine.

When a "straight" person would come backstage there would be some raised eyebrows but nothing was ever said. All seemed grateful for the opportunity to work on the show and a more talented crew I never had.

However this arrangement had its drawbacks. One thing was that in some cases, we found that the fact of most of the crews' sexual predisposition had preceded us and may, in those days, have cost us some contracts. I am glad to see that in 1995 it is not only accepted but boasted about.

Once we needed some girls in a hurry. I went to an old friend of Harry Willard's by the name of George Boston. George was running the "Abbott's Magic Novelty Company" store in Hollywood. He said I should go see Ed Cancino, who ran a top-notch dance studio and always had some girls eager to work. Cancino was a dapper little man who was slight in stature and wore a thin, neatly trimmed moustache. He had dark piercing eyes normally associated with those of Latin extraction. He was very kind and very friendly. He did recommend some young ladies who traveled with us and worked out splendidly.

Hanging on the walls in Cancino's Dance Studio were some

192

pictures of his daughter especially when she had worked with her father as a dance partner. News accounts reflected that they made a very impressive couple of artists. The girl was named Margarita Cancino. Her hair grew too far around on the sides of her forehead. Later she either shaved it off or had it removed by electrolysis. Once the hair was removed and the style and color changed a bit there was a really striking difference. Her eye and lip makeup was changed considerably but when all of the alternations were made she became one of the all time great motion picture actresses and her name became Rita Hayworth.

George Boston had, early in life, decided that he wanted to know all there was about big magic shows. Consequently, he went about the business of hiring on, as an assistant, or any other capacity open, on just about every big magic show of his day. He was a close friend and confidante of Virgil, Willard, Birch, Blackstone, and God knows how many others. Having worked on each of these shows he could spin magic show yarns that would never quit.

Chapter 56

DO'S AND DON'TS

It seems that in today's world we are constantly bombarded with admonitions of "Don'ts." Don't eat margarine. Don't eat meat. Don't eat eggs. First one thing, then another. Then, in due course, we are told that it was all a mistake and it is safe to eat such things after all. It is amazing how those self-appointed guardians of the public gut can be wrong. It seems the human race did a pretty good job of surviving long before the commencement of all this nonsense. Now the latest thing is don't eat salad dressings. The labeling is not true. All salad dressings are bad. Even oil and vinegar. If you eat salad dressing it will give you cancer of the asparagus. To hell with them. Eat whatever you wish 'cause I will guarantee you that you are going to die anyway.

There was a period in our history when showpeople were so frowned upon that many shows, including ours, had the big names of their shows painted out on the sides of their trucks. Some police in small towns would just look for roadshow operators and stop them to shake them down. Some hotel and motel accommodations were closed to theatrical people. In fact many towns had "boarding houses" for entertainers. Such peole were "encouraged" to stay "with their own kind." Those that disobeyed this dictum found prices immedi- ately rose, some outrageously so, restuarants became so slow in

194

waiting on showpeople that they only received service after everyone else. It made no difference that your name was two, or more, feet high on the marquee of the theatre. You were still looked down upon. It had a depressing effect on those brought under such scrutiny. You felt unclean. From the way we were frequently treated, I can well imagine how blacks felt. Even such stellar performers as Lena Horne were forced to use "negro entrances" and restrooms. Why they could not even be served in the restaurants at all.

Chapter 57

WOOLDRIDGE

Willard and my grandfather built a trick for me wherein two tubes approximately 14" square were shown empty. The magician would pick them up, one at a time, and look through them at the audience this convinced of the fairness of the apparatus. The tubes were placed on a tray side by side and the magician would produce a huge number of silken scarves, beautiful fans, umbrellas, and various other interesting objects from each tube. Finally the tubes were again shown empty and one tube was placed inside the other whereupon six white doves appeared therein. The doves were each placed in their cages and the two tubes were lifted off the tray revealing a very large goldfish bowl full of water and live fish.

There was a black magician in San Antonio whom I had befriended. His name was Wooldridge. He always loved that trick. I gave it to him along with some other items... helped him put together a pretty good act. A couple of months later he called complaining that he just could not break into the local entertainment scene. I thought this peculiar because there were so many military bases around San Antonio along with a high number of public and private schools. All of these facilities used live entertainment from time to time. The only place that would hire Wooldridge was the old Eastwood Country Club which was exclusively for blacks. I seemed to be the only local magician who associated with Wooldridge and he profusely thanked me for my help but had decided that he was going to move to Denver. I never heard from him again; but, years later, Tiny Grant, owner of Tiny's Magic Company, told me that Wooldridge became one of the most successful entertainers in the Colorado territory. Tiny Grant's real name was Ralph Mathessen and he did construct, and purvey, some really excellent magical apparatus.

Chapter 58

WONDER DOG

Wonder Dog was half Cavalier King Charles Spaniel and half Scottish Terrier. To fill the void in my life following the demise of my mother, my closest friend brought him to me. I think that the feeling was mutual because Wonder Dog loved me immediately... and I him. He was my constant companion for 16 years. He slept at the foot of my bed every night of his life. He ate what I ate. He had the finest medical care available. During his lifetime he had many surgeries and survived them all. To illustrate the way he thought, let me tell you about the Quality Inn in Arlington, Virginia. We arrived at the Motel very late following a full evening performance. We did not have a reservation and all the rooms were taken except one. That was the room right next to the desk and the manager's office. I went in to register, where I saw posted directly beneath the registration desk a sign which read, "NO PETS ALLOWED." The doves, ducks, rabbits, etc. were well enough insulated in the back of our big truck that they would be alright; however, not Wonder Dog. He was a member of the family. He lived as such and was treated as such. I took the room. I went out and told my wife that she should go in and open a window and I would hand her Wonder Dog through it. That is what we did. Now every other place that we stayed, over those 16 years, when the time came to leave in the mornings, Wonder Dog would run over to the door of the room and, quite literally, bounce up and down like a lamb, until we let him out. By now he was eager to do his business. On the morning in question instead of his running over to the door, he ran over to the window. He knew that was the way he came in and, therefore, that was the way he must exit.

Wonder Dog had a particular job on the show. Whenever a rabbit escaped, which was often, Wonder Dog would be on him in a flash. He never hurt a bunny in all those years. He would merely run down the rabbit and stand there pinning the rabbit down with his nose until one of us came and picked the bunny up and put him back in his cage.

He dearly loved to stand up on the front seat and play like he was driving the truck. He had his own blanket. When on stage he would lie down and never make a sound. As soon as the show was over, he would start raising hell to go outside. He would never even consider causing a problem or making a noise during a performance. Our Veterinarian friends thought it a miracle that he lived as long as he did and attribute it only to the best care they had ever seen given a dog and the love which we heaped upon him.

Wonder Dog died a natural death... just old age. The void left by his departure was so terrible that I have never recovered from it... never will. Little Annie, our cat, came for months after the death of Wonder Dog and put her little head on the pillow beside me at night and she would moan to let us know how sad she was.

I could not bring myself to face the prospect of another dog unless, or until, somehow that marvelous combination breed could ever, by accident, turn up again. It did. A lady who raises Cavalier King Charles Spaniels left her gate open one night and her little girl Spaniel was paid a visit by the little Terrier next door. From that union came two little ones that have almost taken Wonder Dog's place. They are so smart and so beautiful. You would never think that they came from the same litter. The little girl, Ginger, is blond and looks like the typical Spaniel and the little boy, Tuxedo, looks like the Scottish Terrier. We named him Tux because his all black coat and his white chest and goatee makes him look like he is dressed in a tuxedo. I see so much of Wonder Dog in each of them that I cannot help but believe that somewhere, in the long ago, they stemmed from the same ancestors.

199

We have an outdoor cat that always spends the days out and the nights in. He has his special quarters, air conditioned for the summer heat and specially heated for the cold winter. His name is Fraidy. Before he came to live with us we had his twin named Slim. Slim was so lovely and, without any warning, died from heartworms, with no known symptoms. Prior to Slim, Miss Kitty-Kitty adopted us and filled the role of our outdoor/indoor kitty... I had a fur-lined jacket which she fell in love with. I gave it to her and made her bed with it in her special quarters. Oh, how she loved that coat. It was hers and her daddy had given it to her. She would fight anyone that even touched it. She would have been so happy just to lie there, on it, for the rest of her life. She died one night the same as Slim and we have always suspected from the same illness. God, I wish they would find a cure for heartworms for cats. They have one for dogs but it does not work on cats.

Wonder Dog seemed to have a really uncanny ability to perceive and remember certain things. He would check in a motel with us and only see the room once. Still when we went out to eat and returned he would jump down and run to the door of our rooms. From that long line of doors, each exactly the same, he knew which was ours; but, we always had to look at the room key to remind us of the number. He was a great burglar alarm. Once while appearing at Ft. Hood in Killeen, Texas, we were staying at the only nice motel in town. What we did not know was that, being in an Army town, all of the motels were frequent habitats of hookers. A knock on the door sent Wonder Dog into a frenzy and the poor call girl who was standing there when my wife opened the door almost went into shock. Very often in the middle of the night someone would try to open the doors. I suppose this was to see if they could "luck out" and find one open. Boy the miscreants never tried our door twice because Wonder Dog went for them.

If my wife, or I, happened to be on the bed and someone else came near, even a close relative, Wonder Dog would become furious; and, if that person did not leave he would attack. He truly felt like he was our guardian... and he really was.

Chapter 59

THE NARCOLEPTIC MUMMY

Bill McMillan was a very nice looking, blond headed, young man with above average height. He came to work on the show in Corpus Christi, Texas. He was to participate in the performance by playing the role of the Mummy.

We had been successful in obtaining the copy of Lon Chaney, Jr.'s head from his movie role as "Kharis the Living Mummy." We would have an actor put on the canvas outfit actually covered with grey bandage and a zipper up its back. Then some of the young people on the show would go over him with more, loose, rolls of the bandages to tighten it up and cover the zipper. When finished, he would put on grey rubber gloves covered with grey facial putty and the Chaney head.

When the Mummy was to make his appearance, he did so from the Mummy Case illusion. This is a trick wherein an upright rectangular cabinet, on a platform with wheels, is rolled out on stage and the front door opened. Inside the front door were two more doors each opening outward. These inner doors were painted and decorated to look like a sarcophagus. Finally the back door was opened and the audience could see all the way through the cabinet to the back curtain. The back doors were closed, then the inner doors, and lastly the front. All lighting was extinguished, except for a green spotlight, and the doors slowly opened to reveal the Mummy. He just stood there. Then one eye popped open and out he came. The mummy headed right for the audience, all of the lights went out, and the ghost seance began.

Well, we had trouble with Bill McMillan from the start. It was getting him to wake up. We would go to his room and knock until our hands were raw. Usually we would be forced to find a housekeeper and have her unlock his door and then go in and literally shake him awake. This became more and more of a problem. Finally, one night, the doors opened on the mummy case but the mummy did not open his eye. He just stood there; he did not move. I kept whispering, as loud as I dared, "Wake up, Bill... come on." I never did arouse him. We closed the curtain. We knew he was not dead because we could here him snoring.

We called Mrs. Clara McMillan, Bill's mother, long distance and told her we were going to have to send him home and would she please meet the bus. She did not know he was with us and asked us to please not let him out of our sight. She would leave right away and come for him. When she got to the bus station it was obvious that the poor lady was frantic. She said that she had endured really horrible problems with Bill for a long time. Various doctors had diagnosed him with narcolepsy and others said it was neurological. One even said he thought Bill may have a brain tumor. She promised to let us know what they found out in a local hospital and, whether or not, we could be of any help. She never called. When I tried to reach them, their telephone had been disconnected and I never heard from them to this very day. A tragic situation. It is really interesting to note that he did manage to stay with us for several weeks and he did seem to enjoy himself very much.

Chapter 60

COSTUME TRUNKS

The costume trunk is a great old illusion. Let me explain the effect to you and then give you some explanations concerning the methodology.

When the curtains open there is a table type platform with casters on the legs at center stage. This "base," as they are called, is about five feet long and three and a half feet wide. On the front and side edges of this "base" there is moulding type trim and it looks, to the audience, to be about five inches thick. The "base" widens in the center like a pontoon. The entire affair is covered with black velveteen and, up against a black backdrop, certainly gives one the impression that it is not deep enough to conceal a human being. It does NOT contain a person. It does house one half of a person. What I mean is that if someone is lying on their side, with their knees drawn up almost to their chin, and you could draw a line right down the exact center of that person's body, you would find that half of the person was inside the "base" and the other half was sticking up above the top edge. You might well ask why the audience does not see the part above the table line. That is simply because there is one of the four trays of costumes, out of the trunk, sitting on top of the table. This tray has no bottom. There are some parts of costumes loosely strewn on top of the hidden assistant. The other three trays are sitting at odd angles on top of the "base." The trunk has no bottom and it is freely shown to the onlookers. Then the bottomless trunk is carefully lifted up and lowered over the tray of concealment. The lid of the trunk is open and the additional three trays are, one at a time, placed inside the trunk and the lid is closed. A stand holds four different dolls, each dressed with a corresponding costume to the adult size costume in the trays. The magician takes a rifle down into the audience and hands it to a spectator who is instructed not to tell anyone which doll he selects, but to take aim and shoot the doll. He does so and the very instant that he knocks over one of the dolls, the lid of the trunk pops open and out steps the young lady dressed in the costume which matches the selected doll. The dolls are arranged in such a manner that only one doll can be knocked over. This "gimmicked" doll has a piece of black fishing cord running from it to an assistant backstage. The rifle is loaded with blanks and when the gun goes off it is just a matter of the string being pulled from backstage to cause the doll to fall.

Willard never was satisfied with this version of the trick as I have just explained it, although he had three of them. He went about constructing one that worked entirely differently. The base upon which sat the trunk was not tricked in any way. It was just a plain table five feet long and three feet wide. It was only about one and a half inches thick. He figured out the fact that if a girl laid upon this table, knees drawn up but with the upper shoulder turned down as much as possible and her head sideways and flat up against the table, when the bottomless tray was sitting there over her and a pile of loose costumes thrown, casually over her and three other trays beside and by her, that she would neither be noticed nor seen. Other than that the trick worked exactly as did the others except that even magicians "in the know" were dumbfounded.

To see a really big magic show unloaded and uncrated looked like the worlds biggest jigsaw puzzle. Sometimes parts of illusions would be laying all the way up the aisles in the theatres as the show was being assembled. It got to the point that I felt like we were simply well-paid furniture movers.

Two girls named Carol and Ruth came to work on the show. They joined us in Anniston, Alabama, and remained that entire season. Ruth had dark hair and was very shy, withdrawn, quiet, and somewhat colorless. Carol was blonde and gregarious, outgoing, and talked too much. As time passed, a very strange transposition took place. It was almost as though they changed places. Ruth started tinting her hair, changed makeup, became more talkative, laughed, joked, and flirted; whereas, Carol used less and less makeup, darkened her hair, quieted down, and became really a "wall flower." I could never understand what brought about the transposition.

There is a trick that is frequently seen in carnival side shows. It is called a "blade box." This thing is a box just long and wide enough to hold a woman. There are slots cut in the top and matching ones in the bottom. A lady is placed inside in a horizontal position and the lid is closed. Metal blades about 12 or 14 inches wide are pushed down through the top and are left sticking out of the bottom. It is an impossible looking item. It seems as though no one could be inside because there is just not enough room between the blades. Still, in truth, the young lady really is in the box and she is sort of coiled around the blades like a snake. By laying on her side and bending in a peculiar position, she can barely escape the blades. The people in these sideshows used to allow any spectator who wished to come up on the stage and look inside just to see how the girl had contorted herself to accommodate the hazards. They allowed people to see this for a fee, of course.

Willard and I saw this trick in a little show and we went back, night after night, for four nights until we figured it out. That was because it was not like the ones seen in sideshows. It was different because there really was NOT any room between the five blades to conceal a cat much less a human being. We were so perplexed by this illusion that we returned each day of the show's engagement. It was after the show on the last night that we got a glimpse of the secret. The box which housed the dissected girl had eight 2" diameter legs with heavy duty casters on each leg so that the trick could be rolled about. It was when four men went over to disassemble the illusion that we noticed that it took all four to tilt the coffin-like box over one it's side. Then when they unscrewed the four pipe legs on the front (those nearest the audience) it was all that one of these husky young men could do to lift one of the legs. We had hung around after the show just to try and see, without asking, how the trick worked. We each looked at one another with big grins on our faces at the same time. Those super heavy legs had to be filled with lead. The combined weight offset the leveraged weight of the girl who had been slid out on a rolling shelf to the backside of the trick. This shelf was on small cabinet drawer type rollers. The girl just remained suspended on the part of the box that could not be seen by the audience while the blades were pushed through that box. When the blades were removed the girl was simply rolled back in.

McDonald Birch had a great packing box escape which not only garnered his appearances a lot of free publicity but surely swelled the box office. He would commission a local lumber yard or cabinet maker to construct a solid wooden box that was 36" long, 30" wide, and 30" deep. The box was made of 1"X6" boards. It was nailed together and reinforced with 1"X3" strips. The top was separate and made of the same material. A large sign was painted that was almost as big at the top of the box. The sign would read, "Please examine this box all you wish. Birch the Magician will escape from the box after being nailed inside of it by local volunteers at the _____ auditorium on the _____ day of _____, 19__." The sign was attached to the lid of the box with thumb tacks and put on display a week or two weeks before the show arrived in town. When the time came, the box would be hauled out on stage and banged on all of its sides with hammers to prove its authenticity. Birch got into the box, the lid was placed on, and the volunteers were each given a box of long nails and a hammer. They were instructed to nail the lid on as securely as they could. When this was done a rope encircled the box and was tightly tied. A cabinet was rolled up and around the box. The curtains were drawn and almost immediately jerked open again showing Birch on top of the crate and the rope with its knots intact and the lid still nailed tightly in place.

HOW... well before the show when the box was delivered backstage the helpers on the show carefully removed the thumb tacks and took a skill saw and cut out a section of the lid just large enough for the magicians to pass through. The cut was masked on the underside by the reinforcing strip of wood and the sign covered the cut on the outside. All Birch did was push up on the removable section, step out, replace that section, and sit down on top of it.

Chapter 61

MAX SMELLS

Charles E. (Smokey Joe) Smeltz was the general manager of the Benevolent and Protective Order Elks Number 219 situated at the corner of Navarro and Pecan Streets in San Antonio. He really ran the whole shooting match. He established all policies as they related to the operation of the bowling alleys, the wonderful indoor swimming pool, the lounge and restaurant, and a fabulous ballroom with the largest mirror ball I ever saw. The dance floor could seat 1,000 people when chairs were in place. The bandstand also served as a stage and it had entrances to the backstage area on either side. Since Joe Smeltz was my mother's boss, I always went out of my way to be nice to him; he was always kind to me. He was a very well-liked individual. He had a nephew who really thought he was God's gift to the earth. His name was Maxwell Schmeltz. Most of us sort of nicknamed him Max Smells. He thought that he could do anything he pleased on the first try. The first time he went swimming he believed he should be able to swim across Woodlawn Lake and he damn near drowned. He took up the violin... had two lessons and quit... was not fast enough for him. His father, Eddy, also worked at the Elk's Club. He looked after the several hundred hotel-type rooms which the club rented. Eddy was a sort of handy man that could do plumbing, electrical, and general repair work. I think that is what gave Max the idea that he should be able to do anything because his father was pretty good at whatever he undertook.

Joe Smeltz asked me to give a magic performance for the entire membership and their wives during the course of one of the monthly dinner dances in the ballroom on the 8th floor. Max was there. He got all steamed up over the idea of magic. He decided right then and there that he was to become an instant magician. He came back and said that it all looked very easy to him and that he wanted to do it. Joe Smeltz came over and asked that I teach Max some tricks. That really put me on the spot and I practically had to agree. Bobby Kershaw the bass fiddle player was there and said, "Boy, you don't know what you are in for!" Bobby had tried to teach Max the violin. Max said, "I don't want to do any of the simple stuff that you do... I want the really spectacular hard to do tricks"... I almost choked. I invited him over and I gave him an old set of linking rings, some multiplying billiard balls, a book on card manipulations together with a fanning deck of cards, and some other pieces which I felt he might master with practice. I found out that the word "practice" was not in Max's vocabulary.

The very next evening, when I got home, there was a small box at my front door with the things I had given Max and a note saying that "this junk is just too simple for me and my father is taking me up to a magic store in Dallas where I am going to buy some really professional tricks."

Well I forgot about Max for a while. The next thing I heard about him was that he was giving a performance of "Maxwell's Marvels" at the YMCA which was just one short block from the Elk's Club. I usually went to the Club's swimming pool or game room every afternoon to wait until my mother got off work and we would ride home together so she would not have to ride the bus.

I walked over to see Maxwell's rather startling performance. Before the show began I was very impressed. He had two of the most terrific looking all chrome tables I had ever seen. They were covered with beautiful, new magic equipment. He had a vanishing bunny box, the umbrella trick, a change bag, and a necktie which I assumed he planned to plant on a spectator who would come up and let Max cut up the tie. Then he would, magically, restore it by using a magician's utility change bag (an item which secretly switches its contents) and a square circle.

The bunny vanish is a trick in which a box is seen sitting on a table. The magician puts the bunny in the box (at least that is what the audience is suppose to think). Actually the little door on the top is over a black cloth bag nailed to the lid of the box. When the magician puts the bunny in the box (lid) he immediately takes the top off and hands it to an assistant who, in turn, holds the top so the audience cannot see the underside which is concealing the rabbit. Then the magician takes the whole affair apart and shows each section of the box, individually, to be free of trickery or rabbits. It did not work that way for Max. He did not feel that he needed an assistant. He had a chair with a recessed bottom and he planned to simply toss the lid on this chair and, although it could not lie flat it would fit the part containing the bunny into the area of the chair which would sufficiently hide the rabbit. It did not. He put in the rabbit, closed the little outer door, lifted off the top, tossed it onto the chair where the lid promptly slid off onto the floor. Max did not seem to notice. He continued taking the rest of the box apart. He did not take time to witness the proud spectacle of the cloth side being down on the floor and the rabbit struggling to extricate himself. Max missed the amazing sight of the top literally dancing around and finally off the little stage and down the steps.

All was very quiet. Max was undaunted. He picked up the umbrella trick and rolled it up into an oriental mat which he laid on one of his tables; but in the course of moving something on top of his table, so that it might accommodate the umbrella, he accidently held the mat at a 45° angle and the secret, hidden inner umbrella slid out of the compartment inside the outer umbrella. The second umbrella, which the audience is not supposed to know about, plopped out on the floor. Max just stopped and then went on to his next trick. He forgot to put the necktie on a stooge and decided to go on and do the necktie trick by just picking up the tie, cutting it into many pieces with scissors, dropping it in the bag, and turning the handle for the switch wherein he finally would remove the magically restored necktie. He forgot to turn the handle. He turned the bag upside down and out came the pieces. He stuffed them back in but in the meantime he had, without realizing it, turned the handle and when he stuffed the cut pieces into the bag it just so happened that now all of the pieces AND the good tie were in the same compartment. Then when he turned the bag upside down and pulled out the tie, the pieces and the good tie all came out together. The audience applauded because they wondered where a new tie came from.

Next Max commenced the "cut and restored rope trick." This is a trick wherein the magician takes a piece of white clothesline rope and apparently cuts it in half with a pair of scissors and ties the two pieces of rope back together making one rope again but with a large knot in the middle. The way it is supposed to work requires the tying of a square knot which, when pulled upon, inverts itself and will slide off the long rope leaving the knot hidden in the magician's hand. It looks, to the audience, like a man has cut a piece of rope in half and then, miraculously, put it all back together again. Somehow Max managed to confuse the ropes and did, in fact, cut the rope in the wrong place leaving him with two pieces of rope, of approximately the same lengths, which could not be restored. He tugged and tugged on the rope. The knot would not come off so he just threw it on the chair.

He went on to his final miracle which was the "Square circle." This is a rather large square tube with a pretty big opening on the front so that the inside of the tube can be seen to be empty. The inside of the square tube is covered with flat black felt. A second tube is inside the outer tube. What the audience does not know is that the inner tube has still another tube inside of it. The latter tube is covered by the same black felt and is never seen. It is this last black tube that contains the material that is to be "magically" produced. The magician picks up the outer square tube and looks at the audience through it thereby demonstrating it to be empty. He sits this outer tube down over the inner two tubes and removes the next to the smallest tube and shows it to be empty. He can do this because the inner black tube is invisible and the inside of the outer tube can be seen into throughout the process.   After replacing the middle-sized tube the magician reaches in and starts pulling out all sorts of items including livestock. When Max did it all went pretty well and he pulled out scarves, oriental parasols, fans, a couple of self-inflating balloons and lastly what was supposed to have been a live dove or pigeon. It did not happen that way. He had put the poor creature in the tube first and then piled all of the other items up on top of it. Throughout his show the poor dove lay in there smothering and being rather crushed. When Max reached in and lifted the dove triumphantly over his head, its upper torso just flopped, back and forth, and it was obviously dead. Max made some silly remark like, "Oh, he just decided to take a nap." No one applauded, laughed, booed, or anything else. They just silently filed out. One would have thought that at least one trick would have worked as intended. NONE DID! It reminded me of my first show. I am a pretty bad one for not rehearsing; but, I always did when I knew it was necessary and, besides, Harry always let me know when something was not right. Poor Max did not enjoy that luxury. I felt bad for Max and I went up and told him with time it would get better. There were tears in his eyes but he said, "Like hell it will." I heard from his uncle that he never touched the magic again and that his father finally sold the equipment to Berkie who re-sold it in his magic store. I heard no more of Max for many years. Finally, about 20 years later, I heard that Max had died in a sky diving accident. I have always wondered if he forgot to pull the rip cord or if he committed suicide.

There have been many magicians who made very good money and reputations by screwing up their tricks... one was Frank Van Hoven, "the man that made ice famous" and Carl Ballantine. That was not the case with Max. The others planned to have their things go wrong. Max simply did not plan at all.

Chapter 62

MORE ON BERKIE

Earlier I told you about my dear old friend Louis Berkie. In addition to the magic equipment, he also sold the wooden nickels and novelties. One of his best selling items was a small poster of a very old man whose lower lip overlapped his upper. He seemed to be toothless and unshaven. He was wearing the uniform of an officer in the United States Air Force and a flight helmet. The caption under the picture read something like, "YOU CAN SLEEP SAFELY TONIGHT BECAUSE YOUR AIR FORCE IS ON THE ALERT." It looked very funny. The man in the picture looked something like an older version of the comic strip character "Popeye." These things sold like hot cakes. One day Berkie was contacted from an attorney, I think, in New Mexico, saying that he held Berkie liable for the unauthorized use of the man's picture and was planning to file a lawsuit for damages in which he was going to ask for a great deal of money in the form of a judgement. Berkie is a worrier. This scared him and he was so upset over it that he couldn't even sleep. I discussed it with him and he asked me if there was anything that I could think of that might help because he did not have any form of liability insurance that would cover such a contingency. I wrote the lawyer a letter and had Berkie sign it. I explained to the lawyer that it was a violation of an article in the United States Code which prohibits the impersonation of a member of the American Military and/or a government official... I went on the mention that the unlawful wearing of an official military uniform was a criminal offense and I included a copy of the statue. I further advised that the subject in question had every right to pursue his cause of action in the courts but if he did that Berkie intended to demand, by Writ of Mandamus, if necessary, that the man in the picture be prosecuted for his false representation of a military organization member. I made a few hasty calls and found that the subject had been a janitor in the officer's club and some of the members, while on a drinking spree, gave him a few drinks and then dressed him up in one of their uniforms, put the flight helmet on him, and a photograph was taken in the garb. The attorney must have seen the wisdom in the statements contained in my letter because Berkie never heard another word out of them.

Chapter 63

DOLL HOUSE ILLUSIONS

The doll house illusion is one of the most popular items in all of the realm of magic. It is a little house sitting on a base similar, in nature, to the one represented elsewhere in this book under the heading of the "Goddess & the Reptile" illusion. The house has a false back and floor which hides the girl just as the mirrors do in the "Goddess" trick. The rather large front doors are opened and the inside of the house is demonstrated to be empty. The entire affair is revolved and the roof pops open and a young lady stands up. It is obvious to onlookers that the inside of the house is not sufficiently large enough to contain her much less serve as a hiding place.

As you may have guessed Willard's version of this trick was even more dramatic and mysterious. He had several of them but the one which he liked the best did not sit on a low platform like the one fashioned after the "Goddess." His version really was a doll's house with two floors, attic, all of the furniture, etc... it also sat high on a stand that was, at least, waist level. The secret was in the construction of the house itself. He created this mystery in order to produce a little girl. To look at the house one would think it to be entirely too small to contain the child much less hide her. There was barely enough room for the little doll furniture. Willard was very well schooled in the use of colors. He knew that black areas appear to be much smaller than they really are and that white areas appear larger. The child would sit down in the little house and the downstairs floor was hinged to be let down covering her legs. The back wall was hinged to close in front of the little girl. Her head was in the attic and turned sideways. He could have an assistant hand him a burning flashlight through one of the back windows, secretly under the girls armpit, to convince the audience that they were seeing the true dept of the house. When the upper floors and furniture were removed and the front door closed, all that remained to be done was for the child to simply stand up having the roof part as she emerged. By wearing a flowing white dress it seemed to cover the little house. The stairsteps in front hid the child's knees while seated. The outside decoration was the second main deception because the overall dimensions were obscured by the paint job. Willard presented this trick in a lovely and dynamic way so the audiences loved it.

The "Bangkok Bungalow" was another doll house worth mentioning only because of the audacity needed for its presentation. This was a small house which a little assistant, frequently a girl, would walk on stage carrying in the hand away from the audience. This assistant would lift this little house up and sit it down on a platform, about one inch thick and four feet square, and curtains were closed around the doll house. The curtains were pulled open again and a full-sized lady was seen sitting on top of the house. Believe it or not she actually was inside the house. The weight of a human would make it impossible for anyone to carry it and easily toss it upon the platform using both hands let alone doing it one handedly. Still that is just what happened. The lady really was scrunched up inside the little house but there was a piano wire running up to the flyloft above, over a pulley and down to a heavy weight which compensated for the weight of the lady. This made it easy for most anyone to carry it onstage and toss it up on the platform with the woman inside. It looked so very impossible that those watching were frequently seen scratching their heads incredulously.

Chapter 64

JOHN NOVAK

John Novak is a very intelligent fellow who produced the "Encyclopedia of Escapes," a five-volume set that is published by Mickey Hades up in Canada. This was an exhaustive Herculean task and it would behoove any magician, whether he does escape magic, or not, to read them simply because much of the material is very interesting and could, possibly, be adapted to other things. John is an excellent performer and made several tours for the Bureau of Lectures and Concert Artists. Novak is also a linguist who translated for the Military during the war. He is the only true Bohemian that I have ever known.

I think that Novak gave up on humans when he and his wife divorced. He collects little dogs. Loves them and treats them more like people than animals.

Novak worked on our show. He moved from Texas back to his home state of Ohio many years ago and I have not seen him since.

We attend a Presbyterian church in Richmond, Virginia. Julius is our minister and, I must say, he is the finest preacher I have ever heard. He makes an imposing appearance with his mane of shocking white hair.

Our church, like so many others, particularly those in older neighborhoods, has been experiencing a membership crisis. As its members die off there seems to be little, or no, new blood to replace them. Well, I thought up a scheme to increase attendance and turn Julius into one of the best known, perhaps THE best, reverends in America... maybe even the whole world. It starts with the fact that he, as do most other Presbyterian minsters, insists on wearing one of those black "dresses" that they wear while preaching in the pulpit on Sundays. Ministers refer to them as "robes"... so do judges. Both preachers and jurists look sort of silly in a drab black dress. Black is the color which represents evil, gloom, doom, the underworld. So, it was my suggestion to Julius that he agree to allow us to purchase some pretty, loudly colored, material and then my wife could sew him a lovely outfit using the black one as a pattern. People would come from all over just to see him and his name would be on the lips of multitudes. Do you know that he would not hear of it. I saw that my suggestion was upsetting him... so I dropped the subject... temporarily... then, weeks later I bought a few yards of material that had large flowers on it the size of dinner plates. These were flowers of all descriptions and the brightest colors you ever saw. I took the material to church the very next Sunday and I showed it to Julius. I again asked for one of his old "dresses" to use as a pattern and, I know you are not going to believe this, Julius looked as though he was having apoplexy. He backed away from me and, for just an instant, I felt like he was going to hit me. So I gave up. I am only mentioning this in case one of my readers is having the same sort of problem in their church. If they want to take my idea and use it to bring fame, and maybe fortune, to their place of worship they have my blessing and do not even have to give me credit for it.

1. This photograph is an accurate reflection of Willard the Wizard whose real name was Harry Francis Willard.

To my friend Dan.
Willard the wizard.

Wonderful pencil sketch was done by artist
Bob Dale. We wish to express our gratitude
to Mr. Dale and to The San Antonio Express
News for allowing us to reprint it.

APPENDIX A

2.   Our neighborhood showing the close proximity of the homes of those
individuals reflected in the text. .

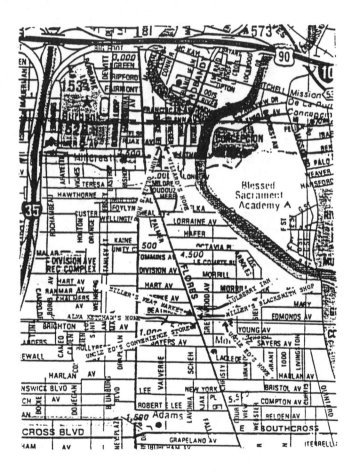

3   Picture of Donald (Estes) Brandon's mother, Nancy Jewell (Miller) Estes.
     Page 22.

4. Pictures of John and Guido Dittmar. This is the only known photo of
    Dittmar the Magician, the only man ever to actually see the Hindu Rope
    Trick and bring the secret out of India with him. He was a member of
    royalty and owner of one of the world's finest magic manufacturing
    companies. He lived in Germany and the United States. The Dittmar
    mansion was located at 505 Howard Street in San Antonio, Texas, and the
    magnificent high rise apartment complex knowns as the Aurora Apartments
    were built and financed by him.

GUIDO DITTMAR, BROTHER OF JOHN

5.   News article from Cassville, Missouri, showing the degree of radical religious fanatic rejection of stage magic.

Group Oppose Magic Event At R-4 School

A group and their pastors representing two area churches, were on the Cassville schools campus last week in opposition to a senior class sponsored magic program. Rev. Floyd Saffell of the Church of God at Golden and Rev. Floyd Renfro of the Cassville Assembly of God, headed a group of approximately 30 persons protesting the show appearance.

Rev. Renfro told the Democrat the group object-ed to advertising circulated by the show. Both he and Rev. Saffell viewed the daytime show for students. Neither attended an evening presentation that was open to the public.

Both pastors conferenced with administrators Superintendent Dan Bailey, high school principal Jerry Marple and elementary principal Eunice Thomas.

The fund raiser for the senior class, for end of school activities, produced about $300 for the cause.

As a part of their protest the group held a prayer session adjacent to the school campus. Both interested parties, school administrators, and protesters echoed the courteous manner in which they were treated.

School officials, who had previously seen the program, said it was recommended for appearance before campus groups by the National Association of Student Councils.

Rev. Renfro said the church objection to the program included some of the advertising material, that it was in a religious form and as such churches were not permitted the same activity on the campus.

Don Stockton, a member of the R-4 board of education, who attended the evening program, said he saw no objection to the program.

CASSVILLE, MISSOURI
WEDNESDAY, MARCH 10TH, 1982

224

6. First Brandon layouts showing news and posters as 24-sheet billboard and letterhead. Produced for Brandon by Charles A. "Kid" Koster, the Dean of American Press Agents.

CHARLES A. KOSTER
Director and Producer

D.L. ESTES
General Manager

HARRY LANDERS
Agent

A LAVISH STAGE
PRESENTATION
BRIMMING WITH
MUSIC, VARIETY
COMEDY AND MYSTERY
ALL NEW
ORIGINAL
DIFFERENT!
ROAD TOURS
EXPLOITED BY
CHAS. A. KOSTER
SINCE 1910
BUFFALO BILL
BARNUM AND BAILEY
BILLY ROSE'S
AQUACADE
MAE WEST
TALLULAH BANKHEAD
BARBARA STANWYCK
FRANK FAY
WALTER HUSTON
LOUIS ANDREWS
EDDIE BRACKEN
JEFFERY LYNN
BILL ROBINSON
BOB HOPE
TOURS 1947-8-9
AND
100 OTHER
BROADWAY
STAGE
ATTRACTIONS

IN PERSON! THE AMAZING **BRANDON** — THRILLS! MYSTERY! LAUGHS! — SPECTACULAR STAGE REVUE — ARABIAN NIGHTS — 1001 WONDERS OF BAGDAD

UNLIMITED THRILLS
CHILLS AND LAUGHS
A MAGIC STAGE
REVUE DESIGNED
WITH THE ENTIRE
FAMILY IN MIND!

ORIGINAL BRANDON LETTERHEAD CIRCA '40's & '50's

"OUR BUSINESS IS TO INCREASE YOUR BUSINESS"

GREATEST PUBLICIZED STAGE SHOW BENEATH THE SUN!

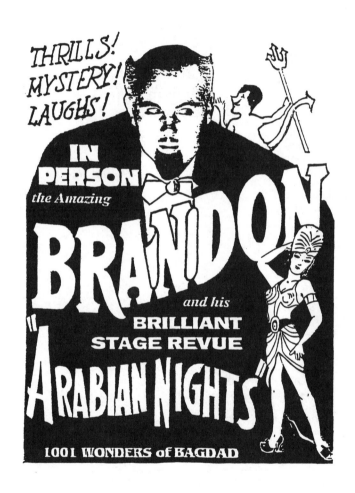

APPENDIX A

7.   Picture of Nancy Langford from Camp Show days.

8.   David Price, Jr., number one magical historian and author of "A Pictoral History of Conjurors in the Theatre" published by Cornwall Books, New York, London, and Toronto. Prime address is 440 Forsgate Drive, Cranbury, New Jersey, 08512. ISBN 0-8453-4738-1. This massive text only covers magic prior to World Ware II but is the most comprehensive coverage of that period. Tells of Willard the Wizard commencing on page 389.

EGYPTIAN HALL MUSEUM

The Wonder Show of the Earth

It's in Brentwood. Interested?

9.   Pictures of Lee Morgan.

Lee Morgan
"The Meanest Man In The Movies"
Veteran Character Actor and Star of 1309 Pictures Will
Appear In Person In Your Theatre During The Showing of

TOMB OF TERROR

Continued on next page--

APPENDIX A

10.   Jack Tiger and Global Productions.

11. "Tomb of Terror" layouts for posters and newspaper advertisements. Reflects evolution.

THIS EVOLVED INTO THIS.....AND THEN THIS

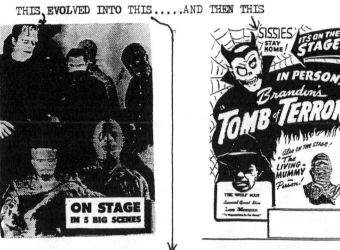

Continued on the next page--

This is the original 40x60 layout done at the same time as
the Devil Vampire head (with the spider web behind his head).
Julius Gordon had his layout artists create this publicity
package for me while I was appearing in his theatres. Julius
was the President of Jefferson Theatres (a subsidiary of
Paramount). The Devil Vampire head was for 14x22 windown cards,
22x28 windown cards, handbills, and 1 col, 2 col. and 3 col news
ad mats.

This 40x60 was reprinted many times. With each additional
printing some of the material relocated such as the Mummy,
Hunchback and Wolfman heads were all down the left hand side
of the poster and the girl saw her hair changed from brunette
to blond. The basic poster remained the same over the years
until Tiger had 2500 of them printed in Stroblite Day-Glo so
that the poster would light up under ultra violet. When a theatre
manager put one of these Day-Glo posters in a dark corner of his
inner lobby with a flashing black light (ultra violet) on it
this thing was startling to say the least. I am pretty sure that
we were the first ones to do this and, perhaps, the only ones.
This poster became so popular that it is in demand today. The
grapevine reported to us that someone paid $100.00 for one up
somewhere near Baltimore. I just simply cannot imagine anyone,
in their right mind, paying for such a thing.

All of the white area behind Frankenstein's Monster was the
bright flourescent red on the Day-Glo version. Various shades
of yellows and greens complimented the black.

Billposters could hang it on outdoor locations as a three (3) sheet
by adding the 20x40 date strip. Sometime they would simply put
a 10x40 white strip at the top and another one at the bottom and
snipe it without the conventional "dater".

Tiger had more printed later on but I was not around at that time
so I do not know what, if any, changes he had made, how many he
had printed or what they looked like.

Continued on the next page--

Continued on the next page--

Continued on the next page--

Joplin, Missouri, 1952

Continued on the next page--

Continued on next page--

Continued on next page--

Continued on next page--

The Very Best of All Horror Stage Shows

12.   Carl Balmer.

PACESETTER attractions

CARL REID BALMER
ARTISTS REPRESENTATIVE
P.O. DRAWER FF
DEL RIO, TEXAS 78840
TELEPHONE A.C. 512—775-4437

CARL R. BALMER

SYMPHONY ORCHESTRAS·BALLET COMPANIES·LEGITIMATE THEATRICAL ROADSHOW PRODUCTIONS

Show-Gram

CARL REID BALMER
ARTISTS REPRESENTATIVE
P.O. DRAWER FF
DEL RIO, TEXAS 78840
TELEPHONE A.C. 512—775-4437

THERE IS NO QUESTION THAT THE AUDIENCE OF TODAY IS MEASURABLY DIFFERENT
THAN LONG AGO. A THEATRICAL COMPANY MUST KEEP PACE AND YET PRESENT
MIND AND EYE BOGGLING EXPERIENCES, IN BEAUTIFUL SETTINGS, TO SEND THE
AUDIENCES HOME TALKING ABOUT THE "LIVE SHOW" AND "THE THEATRE" IN WHICH
THEY SAW IT. THE BRANDON MAGICAL REVUE DOES JUST THAT: RIGHT NOW IS THE
TIME TO ENGAGE "THE LAST OF THE GREAT STAGE MAGICIANS"

YOU KNOW THE PROJECT YOU ARE WORKING ON NEEDS $ MONEY $ IN ORDER TO MAKE
IT WORK. THE BRANDON COMPANY CAN CERTAINLY HELP GET YOUR PROJECT OFF TO
A GREAT START.

OUR OFFICE FILES ARE LITERALLY OVERFLOWING WITH LETTERS OF SATISFACTION,
PRAISE AND RECOMENDATIONS AS TO OUR PROFESSIONAL ATTITUDES, SHOWMANSHIP
AND THE ABILITY TO HELP RAISE FUNDS FOR MANY WORTHY CAUSES DATING BACK
OVER THE LAST 40 YEARS. TRY US...BOOK BRANDON AND COMPANY FOR THE NEXT TOUR
THROUGH YOUR AREA...WE WILL DO A SIMILAR FUND RAISING JOB FOR YOU:

WE HAVE THE KNOWLEDGE AND THE KNOW-HOW TO PUT YOUR ENDEAVOR OVER THE TOP.
YOU WILL BE SO DELIGHTED THAT YOU WILL WANT TO HAVE BRANDON AND COMPANY
PERFORM AGAIN AND AGAIN...EACH TIME WITH AN ENTIRELY NEW AND DIFFERENT
NECROMANTIC EXTRAVAGANZA TO, MAGICALLY, TURN THE CROWDS INTO $ MONEY $
FOR YOU.

THE MAJOR ILLUSIONS, MORE THAN 40 OF THEM IN THE BRANDON REPERTOIRE, ARE
REPRESENTATIONS OF THE GREAT MYSTICS VIRGIL, THURSTON, DANTE AND OTHERS,
WITH SEVERAL IRREPLACEABLE ILLUSIONS OF THE LEGENDARY WILLARD THE WIZARD,
WHO WAS THE MENTOR OF BRANDON, THE LAST OF THE GREAT STAGE MAGICIANS.

BOOK NOW IN ORDER TO BE ON OUR COMPANY'S NEXT ROUTE THROUGH YOUR AREA.
YOU WILL THEN WANT TO MAKE THIS ATTRACTION YOU NUMBER ONE ANNUAL EVENT.
WE HAVE RAISED OVER A $ MILLION $ FOR ORGANIZATIONS JUST SUCH AS YOURS.

REMEMBER, ANYTHING THAT IS REALLY WORTHWHILE IS WORTH WORKING FOR...TICKET
SALES ARE THE ANSWER. THE MORE TICKETS THAT ARE SOLD, THE MORE THAT YOUR
FINE ORGANIZATION EARNS...IT IS THAT SIMPLE.

OUR NATIONAL OFFICE SUPPLIES NEWS STORIES, AD LAYOUTS, A VARIETY OF WINDOW
CARDS, POSTERS, PROGRAM SPACE SALES AND OTHER HIGHLY SOPHISTICATED
PROMOTIONAL ITEMS, ALL DONE IN A VERY FINE PROFESSIONAL MANNER.

IN BRINGING THE BRANDON SHOW TO YOUR COMMUNITY YOU WILL BE DOING A BIG
FAVOR FOR THOSE THAT HAVE NEVER SEEN SUCH A PRODUCTION AND FOR THOSE THAT
NEVER MISSED ONE. OUR EXPERIENCE IS AT YOUR DISPOSAL.

MAGICALLY YOURS,

CARL REID BALMER

SYMPHONY ORCHESTRAS·BALLET COMPANIES·LEGITIMATE THEATRICAL ROADSHOW PRODUCTIONS

241

APPENDIX A

13.   Ken McKinney.

Continued --

243

14. Louis Berkie.

Louis Berkie, The Fun & Magic Shop, and the Elbee Company

APPENDIX A

15. Carl Reid Balmer's death.

Heart attack fatal to Carl Balmer

Civic leader dies, rites Tuesday

Carl Reid Balmer, 63, was dead on arrival at Val Verde Memorial Hospital early Sunday morning after suffering a heart attack. He resided at 206 W. Strickland St.

Rites will be Tuesday at 3 p.m. in the chapel of Humphreys-Doran Funeral Home with Dr. Frank E.T. Kennedy, pastor of the First Christian Church, officiating. Burial will be made in Westlawn Cemetery.

He was born May 11, 1919, in Springfield, Ohio.

Balmer had resided in Del Rio since 1954. He was active in business, community projects and politics. He was a director of the Brown Plaza Association, he served on the advisory board of the Whitehead Memorial Museum, he was a member of Val Verde County Historical Commission, served as chairman of the Cancer Crusade and worked as precinct judge for Democratic primary and for general elections.

Flags at Brown Plaza and at the Whitehead Museum will be lowered to half staff at the time of the funeral.

Through his efforts, the San Antonio Symphony was brought to Del Rio to give concerts on three separate occasions.

Recently he became a member of the League of Historic American Theatres.

He was in business with Bess Huebner at the Frontier Dress Shop until the business was sold.

He had no immediate survivors.

Here from out-of-town for the funeral are Mrs. Sam Simpson and Mrs. Jerry Deakins of Orla, Texas, Mrs. Larry Miller of Houston, Mr. and Mrs. Tom McDowell of San Saba, Mrs. Robert Choate of Dallas, David Graves of San Antonio, Mr. and Mrs. Tommy Graves of Loving, N.M., and Robert Graves of Loving, relatives of Mrs. Huebner.

245

APPENDIX A

16.   Bill Martin's pictures and posters.

THE "MAGIC WORLD OF KARLTON"

- • Is not just an act – it is **a complete production** designed especially for shopping centers
- • The show is successful because it has all of the ingredients of success:
  Action, Humor, Glamour, Intrigue, Music and Originality
- • Attractively staged; Attractively costumed; Attractively priced

We carry our own 20 X 20 stage, spotlights, and all equipment necessary for a completely self-contained show. Our curtains and stage riggings were made by Knoxville Scenic Studios. There are approximately a dozen costume changes in our 20 to 30 minute show. We supply advertising aids, window cards, photographs, advertising art and newspaper stories.

Some of the illusions performed in our show besides the levitation are:

- • The Houdini Trunk Escape
- • Cutting a girl in sixths
- • Doves from nowhere
- • The inexhaustible bowl

Only five magicians have ever been able to perform Karlton's amazing version of levitation.

OUR SHOW WILL PLAY FOR YOU AT YOUR MALL

"The Magic World of Karlton" is now scheduling appearances for 1973.
For complete details, fill out the attached reply card.

Fantasy on Ice — The Unique Iceless Ice Show

PERFORMED ON A UNIQUE
THERMOPLASTIC MATERIAL THAT
WAS DEVELOPED ESPECIALLY FOR
ICE SKATING – NO MESS . . .
EASY, FAST SET-UP – COMPLETELY
SELF-CONTAINED

Karlton
Productions
1213 WEST LABURNUM AVENUE
RICHMOND, VIRGINIA 23227
(804) 355-6321

247

Fantasy on Ice — The Unique Iceless Ice Show

17.   Elmer Deffenbaugh (Russell the Magician).

Diffenbaugh of Mechanicsville, The Amazing Russell, demonstrates a card trick

18.   George Goebel.

George Goebel

One of the all time great stage illusionists

19.　　Ray Mendez.

RAYMOND

20   G.I. Johnson (Moonshine the Magic Clown).

ELASTIC LADY ILLUSIONS

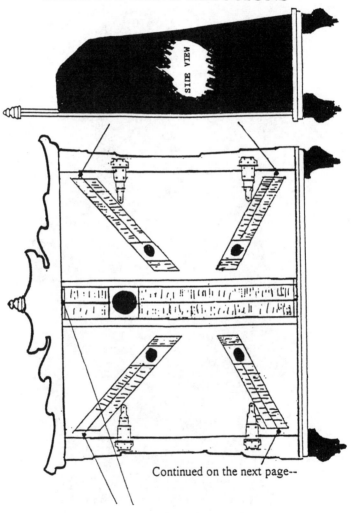

SIDE VIEW

Continued on the next page--

254

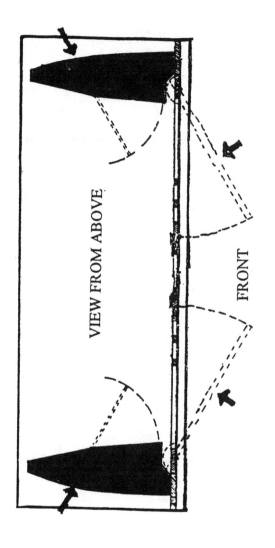

HIDING PLACE FOR GIRL

WHEN FRONT DOORS ARE OPEN THEY HIDE THE SECRET COMPARTMENTS

VIEW FROM ABOVE

FRONT

HIDING PLACE FOR GIRL

Continued on the next page--

WILLARD'S VERSION OF THE ELASTIC LADY

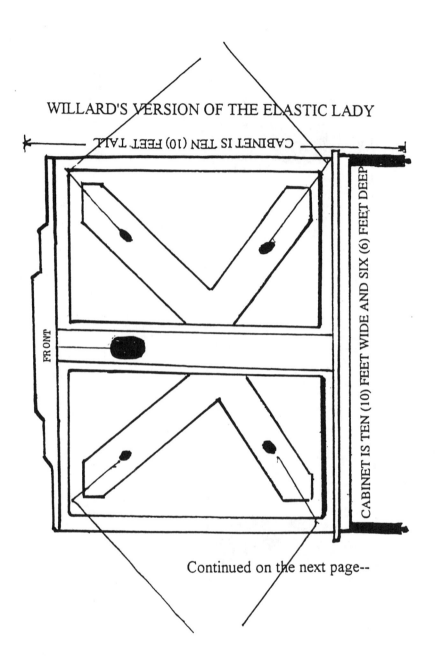

CABINET IS TEN (10) FEET TALL

CABINET IS TEN (10) FEET WIDE AND SIX (6) FEET DEEP

FRONT

Continued on the next page--

WILLARD'S VERSION OF THE SECOND ELASTIC LADY ILLUSION

SECOND PAGE   SIDE OR END VIEW

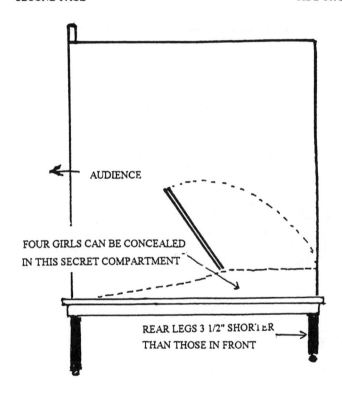

AUDIENCE

FOUR GIRLS CAN BE CONCEALED
IN THIS SECRET COMPARTMENT

REAR LEGS 3 1/2" SHORTER
THAN THOSE IN FRONT

VANISHING BIRD CAGE

The vanishing bird cage is a magic trick wherein the magician holds a brass bird cage, trimmed in red ribbon, between his two hands. The cage does appear to be rigid. In fact it is the magician pulling the ends of the cage in opposite directions that give it the stable appearance. If he were to stop pulling on the ends the cage would, instantly collapse into a condition that would allow it to pass through an opening approximately 1 1/2" in diameter. There is a rope, ribbon, or cord about one quarter of an inch in diameter which runs from the magician's left forearm, or wrist, up his left arm across his back and then down his right arm where, at the right wrist, it attaches to the corner of the bird cage.

By simply letting go of the bird cage and extending his arms in an outward fashion the cage is drawn up his right sleeve and out of sight. This happens so quickly that it simply cannot be seen.

Even the little perch in the cage collapses because it is made out of brown rubber tubing. Some of the entertainers use a real bird. This had been known to kill or injure the canary so most now use a rubber canary which, from a short distance, looks just like a real one.

This "pull" up the sleeve is used for many other tricks including one in which a lady seems to visibly walk through a six-foot length of ribbon which is held by, and between, two spectators.

GIRL WITHOUT A MIDDLE ILLUSION

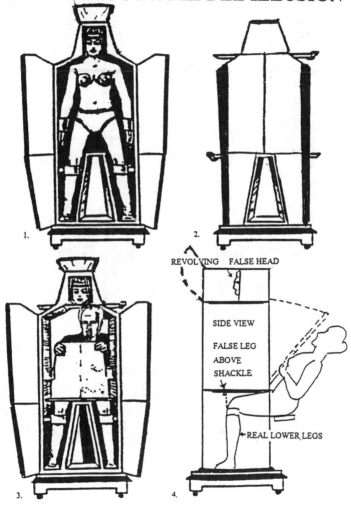

1.

2.

3.

4.

REVOLVING   FALSE HEAD

SIDE VIEW

FALSE LEG
ABOVE
SHACKLE

REAL LOWER LEGS

GLASS LINED TRUNKS

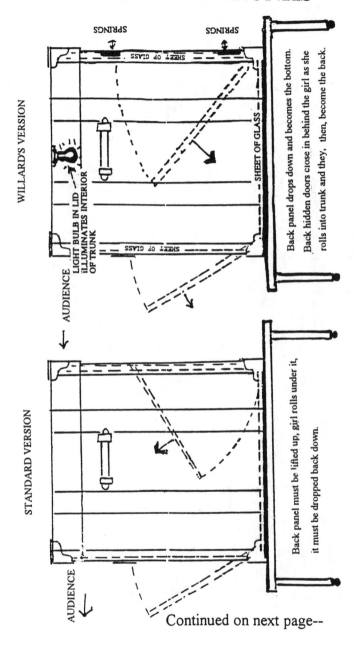

WILLARD'S VERSION

SPRINGS

SPRINGS

SHEET OF GLASS

SHEET OF GLASS

SHEET OF GLASS

LIGHT BULB IN LID
ILLUMINATES INTERIOR
OF TRUNK

AUDIENCE

Back panel drops down and becomes the bottom.
Back hidden doors close in behind the girl as she
rolls into trunk and they, then, become the back.

STANDARD VERSION

AUDIENCE

Back panel must be lifted up, girl rolls under it,
it must be dropped back down.

Continued on next page--

260

Continued --

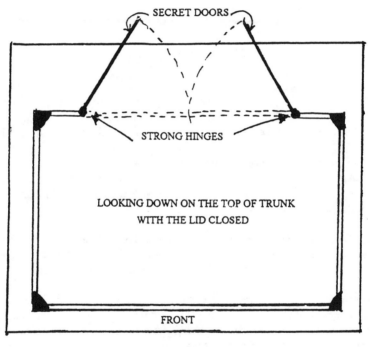

SECRET DOORS

STRONG HINGES

LOOKING DOWN ON THE TOP OF TRUNK
WITH THE LID CLOSED

FRONT

AUDIENCE

261

RAT BOTTLE

This is a great old trick wherein the magician borrows some ladies rings or a gentleman's wrist watch. The borrowed object(s) vanish. The magician offers to try and compensate the spectator over the loss by giving that person a drink of champagne. he pours a rather large glassful from a bottle on his table. After the person drinks the wine (grape juice), the magician takes a small hammer and breaks the bottle open and out pops a live bunny with the lost object tied around its neck with a ribbon. Originally white rats were used instead of rabbits, or occasionally a white dove.

The bottle is made of metal but looks very real. When struck it always comes apart in the same place. The neck of the bottle is sealed off in order to contain the liquid. There are tiny air holes which allow the little animal to breathe.

Willard found a way to use a real glass bottle. He would empty the bottle (you know how) and tie a piece of strong cord around the bottle at the point at which he wanted the bottle to separate. Then, with a large nail, he would tighten the cord like a tourniquet. Before putting the cord on the bottle he would soak it in kerosene. When it was good and tight he would light it with a match. When the cord was burning brightly, he would quickly drop the hot bottle in ice cold water and it would break apart at the string. He would seal the upper part with a cork to hold the liquid.. In the end, he could break the entire bottle up into little pieces and everyone knew it was a real bottle. Today you can buy an instrument just for the purpose of cutting such a bottle.

DIZZY LIMIT (NET VANISH)

NET APPEARS TO BE HANGING BETWEEN TWO PALM TREES WITH A HAMMOCK
TYPE SWING IN FRONT OF IT. GIRL COMES OUT AND LAYS ON BOARD PART OF
SWING. BOTTOM OF NET IS BROUGHT UP IN FRONT OF GIRL ENCASING HER IN
THE NET. A GUN IS FIRED. A FLASHPOT GOES OFF WITH ITS BRIGHT FLASH AND
A PUFF OF SMOKE. THE TOP OF NET DROPS DOWN AGAIN. SWING IS STILL THERE
BUT THE GIRL IS G-O-N-E. Sometimes we would use this same principal in frame and
make a large stuffed animal disappear. It has been used in many ways including the vanish of
a real motorcycle and its rider.

Continued on next page--

FRONT (HIDDEN) NET WITH DUPLICATE SWING ROLLED
UP IN IT... BOTH THE NET AND SWING UNROLL TOGETHER

FLAT BLACK FRAME

SIDE VIEW

AUDIENCE

SWING

PALM TREES

TRIP WIRE

NET ACTUALLY HANGS ON A METAL OR WOODEN FRAMEWORK THAT IS PAINTED
FLAT BLACK TO MATCH THE BLACK VELVETEEN BACK CURTAIN. THE FRAME IS
ALSO HIDDEN BY SOME OTHER COVERING. IN THIS CASE IT HAPPENS TO BE TWO
FLAT PALM TREES. THAT NET, THE GIRL, AND THE SWING NEVER MOVE. THERE IS
ANOTHER NET, SLIGHTLY LARGER THAN THE ONE BEHIND IT. THE FRONT NET IS
ROLLED UP AND HIDDEN, OUT OF SIGHT, DIRECTLY IN FRONT OF THE NET CIRCLING
THE GIRL, THE FRONT NET HAS A PIECE OF BLACK CLOTH SEWN TO IT'S BACKSIDE SO
THAT WHEN IT DROPS THE AUDIENCE THINKS THAT THEY ARE SEEING THROUGH
THE NET ALL OF THE WAY TO THE BACKDROP. A TRIPPING DEVICE ALLOWS FOR
THE NET TO FALL AND WEIGHTS ALONG THE BOTTOM SPEED THE PROCESS.

THE MAGICIAN'S REEL

The magicians reel is a device, never seen by the audience, which is similar to the metal measuring devices that may be purchased in hardware stores. It is much smaller, of course, and it has a strong black thread, or string, instead of the spring metal measuring tape, which can be pulled out and immediately retracted because of a tightly wound spring inside. The magician's reel will instantly retract the thread and whatever object (provided it is light enough in weight) that is attached to it.

DITTMAR'S DRUM ILLUSION

(GIANT ANTIQUE RADIO)

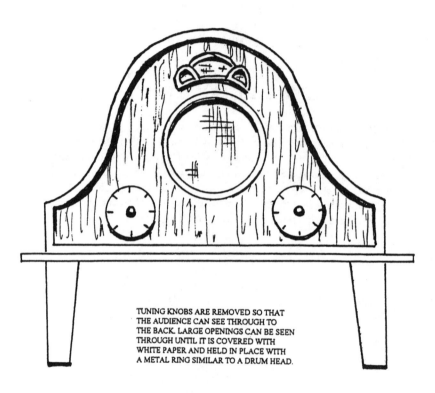

TUNING KNOBS ARE REMOVED SO THAT
THE AUDIENCE CAN SEE THROUGH TO
THE BACK. LARGE OPENINGS CAN BE SEEN
THROUGH UNTIL IT IS COVERED WITH
WHITE PAPER AND HELD IN PLACE WITH
A METAL RING SIMILAR TO A DRUM HEAD.

Continued on the next page--

FRONT

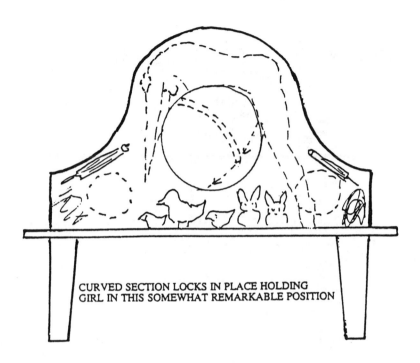

CURVED SECTION LOCKS IN PLACE HOLDING
GIRL IN THIS SOMEWHAT REMARKABLE POSITION

RABBITS, DOVES AND DUCKS ARE HIDDEN IN BASE TOGETHER
WITH HUGE SILK SQUARES... 6'X6', 12'X12', AND 18'X18'.
THEY ARE IN BEAUTIFUL VIBRANT COLORS AND THE
LARGEST ONE COMPLETELY COVERS THE BACKING. THERE
DOES NOT APPEAR TO BE ENOUGH HIDING SPACE FOR THE
SILKS, MUCH LESS THE PARASOLS, ANIMALS AND A LIVE GIRL

GODDESS & THE REPTILE ILLUSION

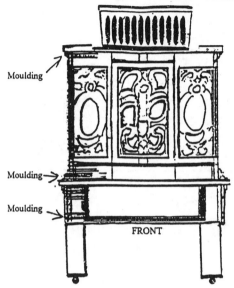

Moulding

Moulding

Moulding

FRONT

GIRL IS HIDDEN BEHIND
THESE TWO MIRRORS

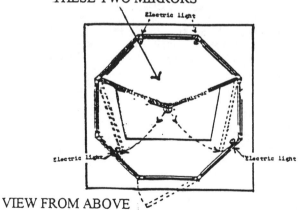

Electric light

Mirror Mirror

Electric light   Electric light

VIEW FROM ABOVE

Continued on the next page--

SIDE VIEW

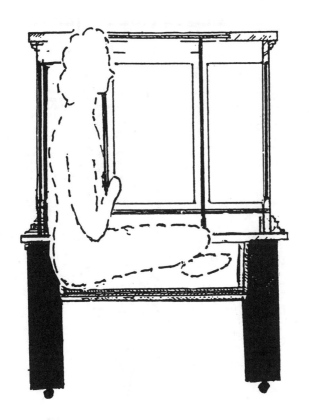

APPENDIX B-10

ELEPHANT/LEAR JET
AIR PLANE VANISH

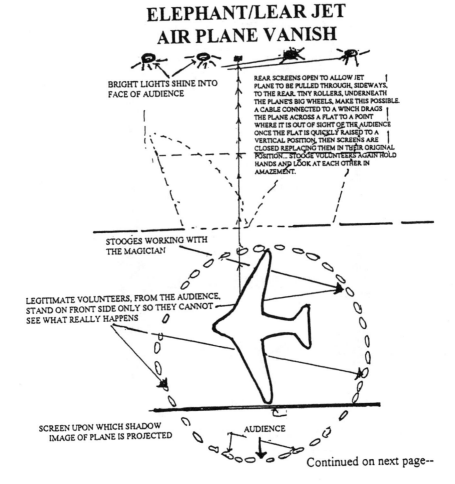

BRIGHT LIGHTS SHINE INTO
FACE OF AUDIENCE

REAR SCREENS OPEN TO ALLOW JET
PLANE TO BE PULLED THROUGH, SIDEWAYS,
TO THE REAR. TINY ROLLERS, UNDERNEATH
THE PLANE'S BIG WHEELS, MAKE THIS POSSIBLE.
A CABLE CONNECTED TO A WINCH DRAGS
THE PLANE ACROSS A FLAT TO A POINT
WHERE IT IS OUT OF SIGHT OF THE AUDIENCE
ONCE THE FLAT IS QUICKLY RAISED TO A
VERTICAL POSITION, THEN SCREENS ARE
CLOSED REPLACING THEM IN THEIR ORIGINAL
POSITION... STOOGE VOLUNTEERS AGAIN HOLD
HANDS AND LOOK AT EACH OTHER IN
AMAZEMENT.

STOOGES WORKING WITH
THE MAGICIAN

LEGITIMATE VOLUNTEERS, FROM THE AUDIENCE,
STAND ON FRONT SIDE ONLY SO THEY CANNOT
SEE WHAT REALLY HAPPENS

SCREEN UPON WHICH SHADOW
IMAGE OF PLANE IS PROJECTED

AUDIENCE

Continued on next page--

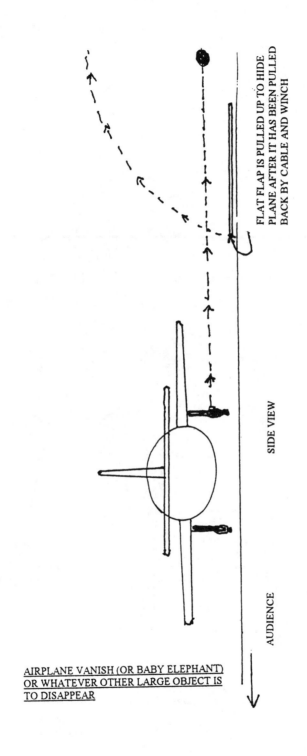

FLAT FLAP IS PULLED UP TO HIDE PLANE AFTER IT HAS BEEN PULLED BACK BY CABLE AND WINCH

SIDE VIEW

AUDIENCE

AIRPLANE VANISH (OR BABY ELEPHANT) OR WHATEVER OTHER LARGE OBJECT IS TO DISAPPEAR

271

TIP OVER BOX ILLUSION
aka WILLARD'S MONKEY SWITCH ILLUSION
aka RAGGEDY ANN ILLUSION

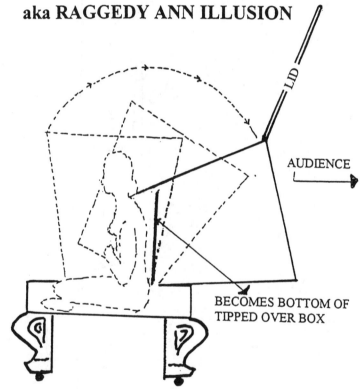

LID

AUDIENCE

BECOMES BOTTOM OF
TIPPED OVER BOX

ADDENDUM

I have received many inquiries of late asking how it could be possible for a magician to create a snowstorm in the audience in a theatre or auditorium. There seems to be a number of ways this might be accomplished. I think that the following is probably the simplest.

There are two mechanical instruments each created to accomplish the opposite of one another. One is a dehumidifier. This machine takes moisture out of the air. Usually the water siphoned out of the humid air is much more than one would imagine. Then there is the opposing machine which is designed to put moisture into the air. This is very good for people who find it difficult to tolerate very dry air. These humidifiers insert large amounts of H_2O, rapidly, and it is blown out in a gush. Well, if a person were to take several of these larger commercial units that do humidifying work and place them in strategic locations in the upper balcony or dome of the theater and turn them on to the maximum, this seeming phenomena could be produced by simply opening the valve on canisters of pressurized liquid nitrogen. The stream of liquid nitrogen would have to be released directly into the moist air. When the nitrogen and moisture collide snowflake particles are the result. This would actually make a snowstorm indoors and over the heads of the audience.

APPENDIX C-1

SOME OF ROLLA ESTES NEFARIOUS EXPLOITS

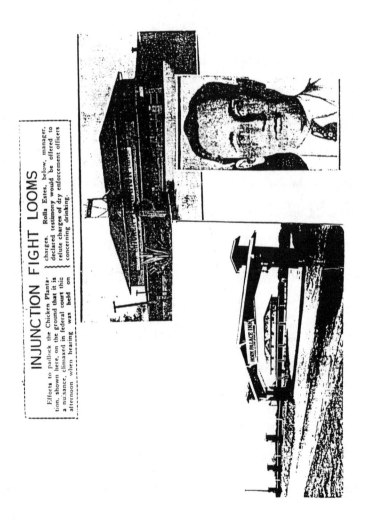

INJUNCTION FIGHT LOOMS

Efforts to padlock the Chicken Plantation, shown here, on the ground that it is
a nuisance, climaxed in federal court this
afternoon when hearing was held on

charges. Rolla Estes, below, manager,
declared testimony would be offered to
refute charges of dry enforcement officers
concerning drinking.

JOYCE (CREPS) BRANDON WAY BACK WHEN. . .

APPENDIX C-3

JOYCE (CREPS) BRANDON AND WYMAN BAKER (DR. SILKINI)

APPENDIX C-4

THE IDIOCY OF THE ENTIRE PROHIBITION SCHEME IS DEMON-
STRATED HERE WITH THIS PHOTO OF A BANQUET FOR THE
CITY COMMISSIONER BY ALL 22 FIRE CHIEFS. ALCOHOLIC
BEVERAGES WERE PLENTIFULLY SERVED TO ALL.

ALAMO DOWNS RACETRACK AT SAN ANTONIO, TEXAS, OPENED IN 1933 SEVEN MILES OUT CULEBRA ROAD WITH STANDS SEATING 5,000 PEOPLE, 16 STABLES, A CLUBHOUSE AND RESTAURANT. PARI-MUTUAL BETTING WAS ONLY LEGAL IN TEXAS FROM 1933 TO 1937 WHEN THE LAW WAS REPEALED.

BRANDON'S FAMILY...LEFT TO RIGHT...AUNT DRUSSIE MCADA, MILTON (THE BUTCHER) MILLER, MARY (KING) MILLER, NANCY ESTES AND CHARLES FRANKLIN (PAPPY) MILLER

SMUGGLERS IN OLD MEXICO WAITING TO PURCHASE THEIR SUPPLIES OF GRAIN ALCOHOL TO FIND IT'S WAY INTO THE UNITED STATES DURING THE LATE '20'S AND EARLY '30'S

"THE LAST OF THE GREAT STAGE MAGICIANS"
DON & JOYCE BRANDON AND COMPANY

"THE LAST OF THE GREAT STAGE MAGICIANS"
DON & JOYCE BRANDON AND COMPANY

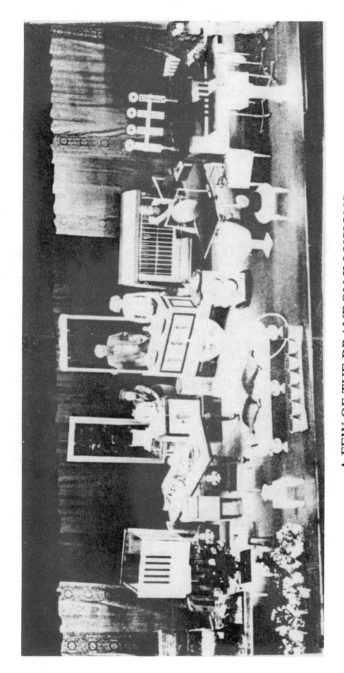

A FEW OF THE BRANDON ILLUSIONS

COSTUME TRUNK ILLUSION

GODDESS AND THE REPTILE ILLUSION

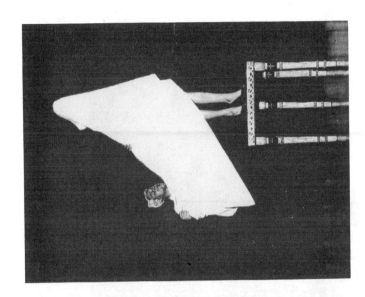

STANDING ASHRAH GIRL VANISH

TIP OVER BOX, aka WILLARD'S MONKEY
SWITCH OR JACK IN THE BOX ILLUSION

LEFT TO RIGHT...CHARLES LOWELL "CHUCK" BURNES, DOROTHY WALKER, DONALD ESTES, JR., EVELYN ROBERTS, AND KENNETH MCKINNEY

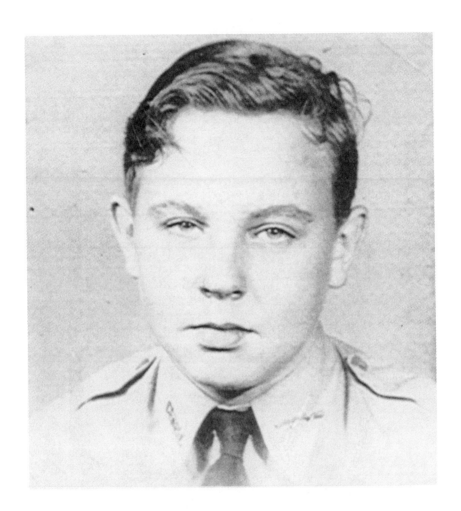

DONALD (ESTES) BRANDON AT AGE 13

LIVE CONCERT AT RICHMOND'S BYRD THEATRE WHICH IS
ONE OF AMERICA'S TEN MOST BEAUTIFUL THEATRES

"THE LAST OF THE GREAT STAGE MAGICIANS"
DON & JOYCE BRANDON AND COMPANY

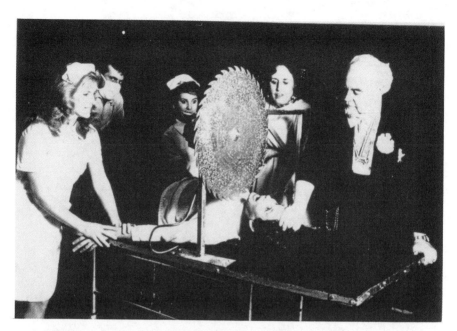

DONALD AND JOYCE
BRANDON
AND COMPANY

PROGRAM

GLOVES TO DOVES
TWO GIANT BOUQUETS OF FLOWERS
MORE FLOWERS?
A SQUARE CIRCLE (AN EMPTY TUBE
   AND SCREEN...OR IS IT?)
MORE FLOWERS
A STAGE FULL OF FLOWERS
AN UMBRELLA AND A PAPER CONE
A BLOOMING BOUQUET...IT BLOOMS
   AGAIN...A BLOOMIN' GOOD TRICK.
MAGIC CHAFING DISH
MULTIPLYING FLOWER
A SOLID CHROME FLOWER POT AND
   ITS COVER

A MISER'S DREAM...ALL KINDS OF
   MONEY FROM THIN AIR

THE SPOTTED CAN
A GREEN FELT BAG
A DUCKS TUB
A BORROWED WATCH
A WATCH GONE...WATCH IT
BY PLAY WITH LINGERIE
CARE FOR A DRINK?
A BOTTLE OF GOOD STUFF
THE WATCH FOUND

THE MIS-MADE SUNSHADE
SILVER LINKS
WHERE DO THE DOVES GO?
SQUARING A CIRCLE
NEXT A CIRCLE CHANGES TO A
   TRIANGLE
ASLEEP IN MID-AIR

INTERMISSION

A SPIRIT MESSAGE
A REAL GHOST...
A DANCING HANDKERCHIEF
THE LITTLE HAUNTED HOUSE
AND EVEN INSIDE OF A JUG
OUT IN THE AUDIENCE...NOW IT IS
"GONE" SIMPLY "GONE"
A LIGHT BULB THAT IS LIGHTER
   THAN AIR
A PENETRATING SWORD...SOLID
   STEEL PASSES THROUGH HUMAN
   FLESH AND BLOOD
THE CREMATORIUMS
NIGHTMARE
THE MAD DOCTOR AND HIS BUZZ
   SAW...IF YOU ARE SQUEAMISH, DO
   NOT WATCH BECAUSE THIS IS A
   SCENE RIGHT OUT OF A HORROR
   MOVIE...ONLY YOU WILL BE
   SEEING IT LIVE...RIGHT BEFORE
   YOUR STARTLED EYES.

HOLLYWOOD'S FAMOUS MONSTER
MOVIE SCENES RECREATED ON STAGE!

SPIRIT SEANCE

THANK YOU AND GOOD NIGHT!

*NOTE-This program is subject to change at any time
without previous notice.

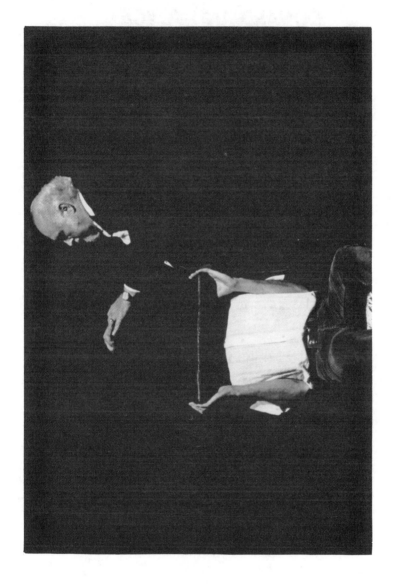

SPECTATOR REALLY "LOST HIS HEAD" OVER THE BRANDON SHOW

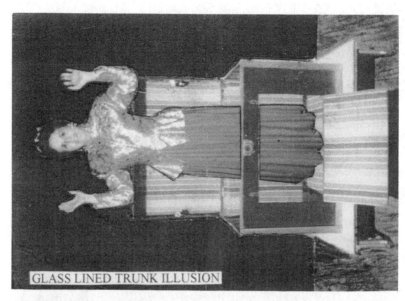

GLASS LINED TRUNK ILLUSION

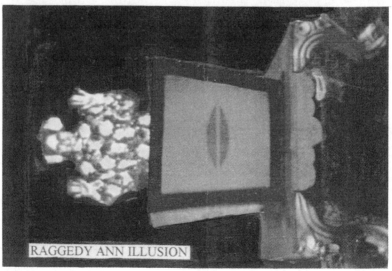

RAGGEDY ANN ILLUSION

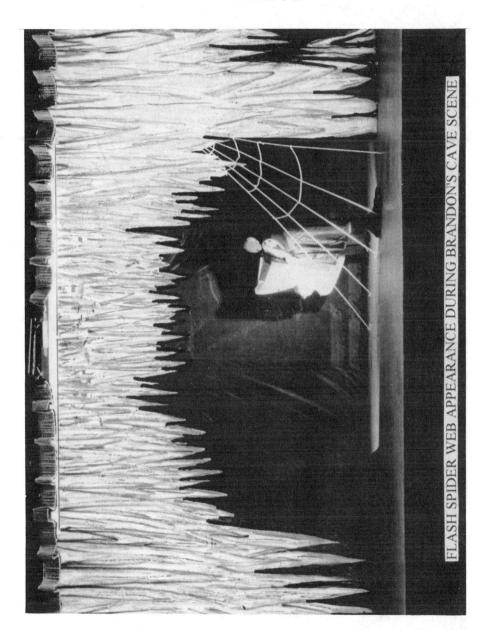

FLASH SPIDER WEB APPEARANCE DURING BRANDON'S CAVE SCENE

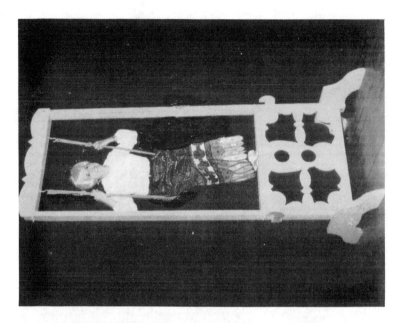

VIRGIL'S ARTIST DREAM

PAGODA ILLUSION

ELASTIC LADY ILLUSION

GIRL WITHOUT A MIDDLE

In the very old copy reproduced here the deterioration demanded that it be restored by computer enhancement and art work.

Sunday, August 10, 1944

THE HOUSTON CHRONICLE

ALEXANDER THE GREAT, magician who opens a three-day engagement at the Uptown Theatre Tuesday.

UPTOWN

FIRST BIG THEATRE ENGAGEMENT AS ALEXANDER BEFORE BECOMING BRANDON

Although there were dinner and dancing clubs with top vaudeville type floor shows, the establishments owned and operated by Brandon's father were, nevertheless, speakeasies whose primary purpose was to serve and sell illegal alcoholic beverages plus offer some gambling. The alcoholic drinks were not served in glasses. They were served in ginger ale bottles with a label around the neck of each bottle like the one pictured below. These bottles were clearly evident on just about every table.

APPENDIX C-29

This is the controversial picture published

by L. B. Company   (Louis Berkie)

SLEEP WELL!

YOUR AIR FORCE

IS ON THE ALERT

APPENDIX C-30

Charles Franklin Miller's first blacksmith's shop (circa 1900)

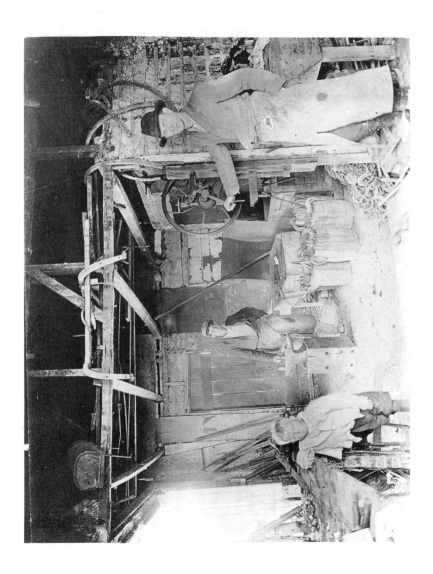

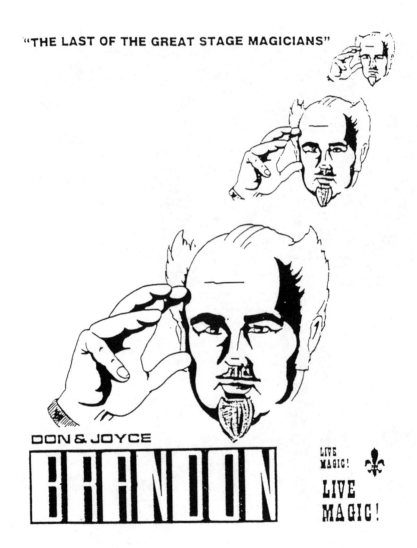

"THE LAST OF THE GREAT STAGE MAGICIANS"

DON & JOYCE
BRANDON

LIVE MAGIC!

LIVE MAGIC!

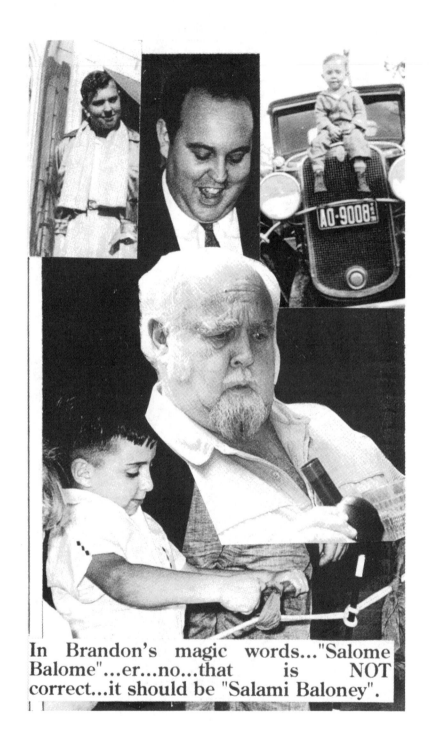

In Brandon's magic words..."Salome Balome"...er...no...that is NOT correct...it should be "Salami Baloney".